Literature-Based Reading Activities _

Third Edition

Ruth Helen Yopp
California State University, Fullerton

Hallie Kay Yopp
California State University, Fullerton

Allyn and Bacon

Boston   London   Toronto   Sydney   Tokyo   Singapore

K.H

To
Tom, Billy, & Danny Edwards
and
Bert, Peter, & Erica Slowik

Series Editor: Arnis E. Burvikovs
Vice President, Editor in Chief, Education: Paul A. Smith
Editorial Assistant: Patrice Mailloux
Marketing Manager: Brad Parkins
Editorial-Production Administrator: Annette Joseph
Editorial-Production Coordinator: Holly Crawford
Editorial-Production Service: Colophon
Composition Buyer: Linda Cox
Electronic Composition: Publishers' Design and Production Services, Inc.
Manufacturing Buyer: Julie McNeill
Cover Administrator: Brian Gogolin

Copyright © 2001, 1996, 1992 by Allyn & Bacon
A Pearson Education Company
160 Gould Street
Needham Heights, MA 02494

Internet: www.abacon.com

Between the time Web site information is gathered and then published, it is not unusual for some sites to have closed. Also, the transcription of URLs can result in unintended typographical errors. The publisher would appreciate notification where these occur so that they may be corrected in subsequent editions. Thank you.

Library of Congress Cataloging-in-Publication Data

Yopp, Ruth Helen.
   Literature-based reading activities / Ruth Helen Yopp, Hallie Kay
Yopp.—3rd ed.
      p.   cm.
   Hallie Kay Yopp appears first on the previous edition.
   Includes bibliographical references and index.
   ISBN 0-205-31963-7
   1. Reading (Elementary)   2. Literature—Study and teaching
(Elementary)   I. Yopp, Hallie Kay.   II. Title.
LB1573.Y67 2001
372.64′044—dc21   00-044797

Printed in the United States of America
10 9 8 7   05   04

Credit: pp. 26–27 from *Where the Readers Are* (pp. 22–23) by C. F. Reasoner, 1972, New York: Dell. Copyright 1972 by Delacorte Press, a division of Bantam, Doubleday, Dell Publishing Group, Inc. Adapted by permission.

10/25/04

Contents _____

Preface_____

Literature can be a powerful force in the lives of human beings. It can make us feel, think, wonder, and understand. It can provide us with exciting, interesting information. It can change who we are forever.

While preparing this edition we read and reread many great books. In fact, it took us longer to write this edition than it should because we found ourselves spending more time talking about the literature we were including than getting our writing done. Our husbands will remember the many late night phone calls we made to each other to share a passage that just couldn't wait until morning. We are awed by the incredible talent of the authors and illustrators whose work we read, and we are sorry that we could not incorporate into this edition all the wonderful books that we talked about in those wee hours.

We also talked about how much we talked. We personally witnessed the importance of sharing books with peers. We interrupted each other's thinking and writing (and sleep and dinners . . .) many times to share one more reaction to something we had read. We wish for all children this same joy in reading and the same opportunities to share their responses with important people in their lives, including their classmates and their teachers.

This book is for teachers. As educators and as parents, we know how important you are. You influence our children every day with the decisions you make—decisions to share good books, decisions to provide meaningful experiences, decisions to listen. We hope the ideas in this book will support you in providing thought-provoking experiences that respect and value the students in your classrooms.

The organization of this book remains the same as in previous editions. Chapter One provides background for the activities we share in subsequent chapters. Chapters Two, Three, and Four provide descriptions of numerous activities for literature-based reading experiences. Each activity may be used at any grade level; we have used them with kindergarten through university students. Examples are provided from a variety of genres, including folktales, fantasy, realistic fiction, historical fiction, poetry, biography, and informational books. This edition offers six new activities, some twists on old ones, and many examples from books we have not shared before.

Chapter Five provides suggestions for constructing individual and classroom books. A few important final comments are offered in the Afterword. Lists of professional journals and Web sites that provide information on children's literature and titles of Newbery, Caldecott, and Orbis Pictus award winners are included in appendices.

We wish to acknowledge the following reviewers who provided helpful comments about the book: R. Jeffrey Cantrell, University of Scranton; Irene Martinez Mosedale, Plymouth State College; Patricia Scanolon, University of Wisconsin, Oshkosh; and Sandra Troyer, Saddleback Valley Unified School District and University of California, Riverside.

We are grateful to the following people for their contributions to this book: Nancy Brewbaker, Paula Gray, and Alan Saldivar, Example 3.20; Doreen Fernandez, Janie Frigge, Kimberly Hennessy, and Thursa Williams, Example 4.3; and Jeanine Rossi, retelling picture book example.

We also thank Arnis Burvikovs, our editor, for his support of this project.

So, Hallie, now that we've finished our writing, I'm off to read Richard Peck's *A Long Way from Chicago*.

OK, Ruth, but first let me tell you about *The Inuksuk Book* by Mary Wallace.

CHAPTER ONE

Using Literature in the Classroom

LITERATURE IN THE CLASSROOM

Although we live in a time of great debate about how best to teach children to read, most educators and policymakers are in agreement that literature should play a role in a child's literacy program. When we examine the goals of literacy instruction—to develop students' ability to learn with text; to expand their ability to think broadly, deeply, and critically about ideas in text; to promote personal responses to text; to nurture a desire to read; and to develop lifelong learners who can use printed information to satisfy personal needs and interests and fully and wisely participate in society—we see the value of using literature in the classroom. How are teachers to stimulate minds and hearts without good literature? How are students to explore ideas, come to understand the perspectives of others, grow in their thinking, and develop a love of reading without good literature? Literature nurtures the imagination; provides enjoyment; and supports exploration and understanding of ourselves, understanding of others, and of the world in which we live. Without authentic and compelling texts and meaningful instructional contexts, quality literacy instruction cannot happen (Raphael, 2000) and we cannot achieve the goals that we hold dear.

Research has shown that literature supports literacy development in a variety of areas. It facilitates language development in both younger and older children (Chomsky, 1972; Morrow, 1992; Nagy, Herman, & Anderson, 1985). It increases reading comprehension (Cohen, 1968; DeFord, 1981; Feitelson, Kita, & Goldstein, 1986; Morrow, 1992; Morrow, O'Connor, & Smith, 1990). It positively influences students' perceptions of and attitudes toward reading (Eldredge & Butterfield, 1986; Hagerty, Hiebert, & Owens, 1989; Larrick, 1987; Morrow, 1992; Tunnell & Jacobs, 1989). And literature influences writing ability (DeFord, 1981, 1984; Eckhoff, 1983; Lancia, 1997) and deepens knowledge of written language and written linguistic features (Purcell-Gates, McIntyre, & Freppon, 1995).

Teachers include literature in a variety of ways in their programs, ranging from teacher-led, whole-class experiences with a teacher-selected book, to small, temporary student-led groups with each group reading a different student- or teacher-selected book, to independent reading of self-selected books. Hiebert and Colt (1989) argue that each of these patterns of instruction contributes to and is necessary for effective literacy instruction. Teacher-led, whole-class experiences provide students with the guidance they need to become expert readers and the opportunities they need to gain alternative points of view necessary for building and revising understandings of text. Small student-led group experiences provide students with opportunities to participate and to attain social and interpretive authority in a setting safer than a whole-class experience. Indeed, Raphael (2000) found that often students who are reluctant to speak in whole-class or teacher-directed situations are more forthcoming in small groups about difficulties they are experiencing with text. Individual reading of self-selected books respects student interests and choice and helps students develop the independent reading strategies that underlie lifelong reading.

The importance of providing opportunities for students to interact with peers about literature cannot be overstated. Current thinking among literacy experts is that building understandings of a text is a collaborative effort (Beck, McKeown, Hamilton, & Kucan, 1997) and that interactions among students are crucial to engaging them with text ideas and developing their understandings about ideas in books and their ability to think (Langer, 1995). While classroom discussions have long been a part of literacy instruction, traditionally those discussions have been highly centralized—the teacher decides what the students will talk about and orchestrates the discussion. This type of discussion may serve to inhibit students' willingness to fully express themselves. Recently, a more decentralized view has been advocated (Almasi, 1995, 1996; Jewell & Pratt, 1999; Langer, 1995; Wiencek & O'Flahavan, 1994). In this view, discussions are guided by students' responses to a book. The students talk to each other rather than to the teacher, and varied perspectives and opinions are valued, explored, and challenged.

This respect for students' personal responses to literature has roots in Rosenblatt's reader-response theory. According to Rosenblatt (1991), readers need to develop the ability to read efferently and aesthetically; that is, they need to be able to gather information from the text as well as to experience the text. Teachers, of course, can and do influence students' interactions (or transactions, as Rosenblatt [1978] calls them) with text. If teachers focus on the information in a text during and after the students read or listen to a selection, teachers are promoting an efferent stance: students learn that they read in order to gather and remember information. If, on the other hand, teachers encourage enjoyment of the reading experience and prompt personal responses to the reading; if they ask students to recapture the lived-through experience of the reading through drawing, dancing, talking, writing, or role playing; if they allow students to build, express, and support their own interpretations of the text, they are promoting an aesthetic stance on the part of the students. Traditional classroom discussions tend to promote a predominantly efferent stance, while more current suggestions for classroom discussion practices support aesthetic responses as well.

The purpose of this book is to assist teachers in providing meaningful experiences that support students' engagement with literature. We offer a variety of activities that are open-ended, encourage critical thinking and discussion, focus on ideas in text, and stimulate personal responses to literature.

First, we present a brief list of teacher responsibilities that are critical to the successful use of literature in the classroom. Then we identify questions that guided our search for activities to include in this book.

TEACHER RESPONSIBILITIES

1. *Know children's literature.* Familiarize yourself with a wide variety of children's literature, and keep abreast of newly published works. Spend time in libraries and bookstores. Explore Web sites that provide lists of award-winning literature, reviews of children's literature, and ideas for using literature. (Some of these Web sites are listed in Appendix A of this book, and recipients of three major awards—the Caldecott, the Newbery, and the Orbis Pictus—are listed in Appendix B.)

2. *Provide students with access to a wide variety of children's literature.* Develop a rich classroom library that includes selections reflecting a wide range of interests, topics, and difficulty levels. Be sure to make available a variety of genres, including informational books, which are a scarcity in many classrooms (Duke, 1999; Yopp & Yopp, 1999; Yopp & Yopp, 2000).

3. *Provide time for students to read.* There is widespread agreement that time spent reading is key to reading development (Anderson, 1996; Cunningham & Stanovich, 1998; Fielding & Pearson, 1994).

4. *At those times when you choose to provide group experiences with a particular piece of literature, be sure to read the book.* Simple as it may seem, it is extremely important prior to engaging students in a literature experience that you read the entire book yourself. It is not possible to plan meaningful experiences or respond to students' explorations without being familiar with the book.

5. *Identify themes in the book.* Many books have multiple themes. *Island of the Blue Dolphins* by Scott O'Dell, for example, examines loneliness, traditions, and survival. These themes will guide the experiences you plan for your students. Be prepared for the possibility, however, that during the course of discussion other themes may emerge from the students that will take precedence over the ones you selected.

6. *Plan activities for three stages of exploration: before, during, and after reading the book.* Prereading activities should spark students' curiosity, set the stage for aesthetic responses to the literature, and activate relevant background knowledge. During-reading activities should promote comprehension, support evolving interpretations of the book, and call attention to effective uses of language. Postreading activities should extend students' thinking about ideas, events, or characters in the book and promote connections between the book and real life or between one book and another.

7. *Establish an atmosphere of trust.* Students will honestly communicate their feelings, experiences, and ideas only if there is an atmosphere of trust in the classroom. You can promote trust by listening actively to the contributions of your students, respecting all student attempts to share, and allowing for a variety of interpretations of the meaning of a selection as long as the reader can support his or her ideas on the basis of the language in the text. Disagreements among students will lead back to the book and result in a closer analysis of the author's words.

RATIONALE FOR SELECTION
OF ACTIVITIES FOR THIS BOOK

The following questions guided our search for activities to include in this book.

1. *Will the activity promote grand conversations about books?* "Grand conversations" can be best described by contrasting them to the "gentle inquisitions" that take place in many classrooms (Bird, 1988; Edelsky, 1988). During grand conversations, students are encouraged to think, feel, and respond to ideas, issues, events, and characters in a book. They are invited to express their opinions, and their opinions are valued. Personal involvement with the ideas contained in the book is encouraged, and individual interpretations are permissible as long as they are supported with data from the text. Grand conversations are similar to the discussions that occur in adult book groups in that the focus is on topics that are meaningful to the participants, and everyone is encouraged to contribute.

During "gentle inquisitions," on the other hand, the tone of the classroom interaction is one of "checking up" on the students. The teacher asks questions, and the students answer them. Although it is appropriate to assess students' comprehension, studies have revealed that a great deal of reading instructional time is spent asking students questions for the purpose of assessing their comprehension (Durkin, 1979; Wendler, Samuels, & Moore, 1989), and that higher-level reasoning activities such as discussing and analyzing what has been read are not routinely emphasized for students (Langer, Applebee, Mullis, & Foertsch, 1990). Allington (1994) agrees that children "need substantially less interrogation and substantially more opportunities to observe and engage in conversations about books, stories, and other texts they have read" (p. 23).

The activities provided in this book can be used to stimulate grand conversations. They provide teachers with a structure for encouraging students to express their ideas honestly and share their thoughts and experiences with their peers. Thus, they provide an alternative to the traditional question-and-answer discussion format that usually focuses on correctness, can discourage meaningful conversations, and often limits participation to the most verbal children in the class.

Some argue that the teacher's role in literature conversations is twofold (Gilles, Dickenson, McBride, & Van Dover, 1994; Jewell & Pratt, 1999; Langer, 1995). First, the teacher should help students learn how to participate in discussions by inviting them to participate, making them aware when their ideas are not being understood, and orchestrating the flow of discussion by emphasizing the connections to others' ideas and by extending the ideas being discussed (Langer, 1995). Second, the teacher should help students work through and further develop their ideas and their thinking about the text. This can be done by helping them focus their ideas; elaborate on their ideas; and link ideas from the text, discussion, or personal experience, and by offering them new ways to think about ideas. Langer acknowledges that for many teachers it will be difficult to learn to listen to students' ideas and base instruction on students' responses rather than rely on a lesson plan. However, if students are to arrive at their own responses, explore ideas and alternative viewpoints, and move from initial understandings to more thoughtful interpretations of a text, teachers must make this shift.

2. *Will the activity develop and/or activate background knowledge?* Recent research reveals that a reader's organized knowledge of the world provides the basis for his or her comprehension of ideas in texts. This organized knowledge is referred to as a reader's *schema.* Comprehension is said to occur only when a reader can mentally activate a schema that offers an adequate account of the objects, events, and relationships described in a text (Anderson, 1984). The following sentence offered by Bransford and McCarrell (1974) illustrates this phenomenon: *The notes were sour because the seam split.* The vocabulary is not difficult and the sentence is short, yet it probably makes little sense to you. However, if you have any knowledge of bagpipes and you read this sentence in the context of bagpipes, it is no longer incomprehensible. Your schema of bagpipes accounts for all the elements in the sentence: the split seam, the sour notes, and the cause-effect relationship between the two. Failure to activate, or call to mind, an appropriate schema results in poor comprehension. An effective teacher promotes comprehension in his or her students by providing experiences that encourage them to access relevant knowledge prior to encountering a text. If students do not have the relevant background knowledge, then an effective teacher will help the students acquire the appropriate knowledge.

Many of the activities described in this book, especially those recommended for use before reading, are ideal for activating and building background knowledge. They require students to think about experiences they have had or to articulate their opinions on topics about which they will subsequently read. Students with limited background knowledge on a particular topic will benefit from listening to the comments of peers.

3. *Will the activity provide opportunities for reading, writing, listening, and speaking?* It has been argued that reading must be seen as part of a child's general language development and not as a discrete skill isolated from listening, speaking, and writing

(Anderson, Hiebert, Scott, & Wilkinson, 1985). Listening, speaking, reading, and writing are interrelated and mutually supportive, and classroom experiences must reflect this. Literacy experts encourage teachers to help their students understand the connection among these language skills (DeFord, 1981; Heller, 1991; Holdaway, 1979; Raphael & McMahon, 1994; Shanahan, 1988).

Each of the activities described in this book provides opportunities for the integration of the language arts. None of the activities is intended to be reproduced on paper and independently completed by silent students. Rather, the activities should serve as springboards for discussions and are designed to inspire students to articulate their ideas and listen and respond to the ideas of others. Writing should be a natural outgrowth of the speaking, listening, and reading experiences.

4. *Does the activity promote higher-level thinking?* Many teachers are familiar with Bloom's (1956) taxonomy of educational objectives, a hierarchical classification system identifying levels of cognitive processing or thinking. The levels of the taxonomy from lowest to highest are knowledge, comprehension, application, analysis, synthesis, and evaluation. The lower levels, knowledge and comprehension, involve the ability to recall information and to understand it. The higher levels—application, analysis, synthesis, and evaluation—involve the ability to apply information learned, classify, compare and contrast, explain ideas or concepts, create, and evaluate or judge. According to Bloom (1984), educational practices, including the selection of instructional materials and the teaching methods used, seldom rise above the knowledge level. Similar conclusions were reported in the 1990 NAEP document (Langer et al., 1990) which revealed that students appear to have great difficulty with tasks requiring them to explain or elaborate on what they read, and that activities that promote higher-level reasoning, such as discussing, analyzing, or writing about what has been read, are not emphasized routinely in U.S. classrooms. More recently, Taylor, Pearson, Clark, and Walpole (1999) reported that very small numbers of teachers in their national study asked higher-level questions about reading selections, and that when discussions occurred, which was rare, they primarily focused on facts.

The activities included in this book serve to facilitate higher-level thinking. They provide opportunities for active interchange among students and encourage students to think and write about ideas that have been or will be confronted in the reading selection. They require students to compare and contrast characters and books, diagram relationships, and support their opinions with examples from the text. Many of the activities encourage creativity.

5. *Can the activity be used with heterogeneous groups of students?* Few would argue with the notion that all students should have the opportunity to interact with good literature. Unfortunately, however, in their efforts to meet the needs of less-prepared or less-able readers, some teachers limit these students to short prose and to worksheets and activities addressing only low-level cognitive skills. Poor readers are often isolated from their more able peers and have neither the opportunity to share in a literature experience nor the opportunity to participate in the grand conversations about books that other students enjoy. Indeed, children in low-ability groups have been shown to receive less instruction and qualitatively different instruction than children in high-ability groups (Allington, 1980, 1984, 1994; Anderson et al., 1985; Bracey, 1987; Walmsley & Walp, 1989; Wuthrick, 1990). For these and other reasons, many experts recommend that flexible grouping be implemented in classrooms.

In flexible grouping, students have opportunities to participate in a variety of grouping structures—both homogeneous and heterogeneous. New groups are created frequently and disbanded once the purposes of the group are achieved.

As we previously mentioned, one group structure is the whole class. Another is small heterogeneous groups. Interacting with peers in heterogeneous settings provides important support for students' comprehension (Raphael, 2000), partly because it reduces the limiting effect of insufficient background knowledge as students can draw on the backgrounds of peers to make sense of what they read (van den Broek & Kremer, 2000). In addition, participation in grand conversations with peers of differing reading abilities is important because these discussions provide a window on how others think.

One of the advantages of the activities presented in this book is that they can be easily and successfully implemented with students in heterogeneous settings. Students of all ability levels can participate in the activities. Some students may respond at a higher level than others, but each student can contribute and each can benefit from listening to the experiences and opinions of peers.

6. *Can students who are learning English as a second language benefit from these activities?* Reading instruction should be offered in the primary language of the students while they are learning English. Many times, however, this is not possible due to limited resources in terms of both personnel and materials. Teachers must be careful as they attempt to meet the needs of these children not to isolate them from their classmates during reading instruction or to provide them with only low-level worksheets that emphasize discrete skills. Experiences with literature need not be withheld until students are fluent in English. Instructional practices, however, should be guided by our knowledge of effective techniques for teaching second-language learners.

In selecting the literature activities for this book, we considered what is known about appropriate instruction for second-language learners. Several principles guided our selection (Cummins, 1989; Echevarria & Graves, 1998; Kagan, 1986; Scarcella, 1990; Schifini, 1996; Spangenberg-Urbschat & Pritchard, 1994). First, second-language learners should be provided with opportunities to listen, speak, read, and write in meaningful contexts. The activities included here offer many opportunities for students to share ideas and experiences through discussions and writing. Because they are asked to express their own experiences related to book content, these discussions are interesting and personally meaningful. Further, the focus is on communication. Second, information should not be presented in a strictly verbal format; visual representations of content aid comprehension. Many of the activities described in the book offer visual or graphic representations of themes or content. Third, many minority children perform better in cooperative and collaborative settings that encourage interaction than in individualistic, competitive settings. The activities presented here can be successfully used by pairs, small groups, or large groups. Fourth, instruction should focus on higher-level cognitive skills rather than factual recall. All of the activities included in this book promote higher-level thinking in the classroom. Fifth, modeling is important, especially for individuals learning a new language. The activities provide the opportunity for children to explain their thinking; thus, students serve as models for one another. Sixth, second-language learners are supported when purposes are set for reading. These activities serve to establish purposes before the students read, while they read, or as they revisit the text after reading.

Our comments here address how the activities in this book are supportive of English-language learners' participation in reading experiences. We would also like to point out, however, that diversity in a classroom enriches learning opportunities for all class members as students draw on one another's background experiences, share ideas and interpretations, and work toward communicating ideas with one another. The more diverse a classroom population, the greater the potential that many and varied experiences, perspectives, and interpretations will arise, contributing to richer understandings for all.

CONCLUSION

Literature should be at the heart of our literacy programs. Not only does it support many aspects of literacy development—language, comprehension, writing, attitudes, and perceptions—it provides an excellent context for deep thinking and personal response. Literature inspires us and informs us; it nurtures our imaginations; it moves us to laughter, to tears, and to action. In the remaining chapters of this book, we provide activities that support students' rich interactions with text.

REFERENCES

Allington, R. (1980). Teacher interruption behaviors during primary-grade oral reading. *Journal of Educational Psychology, 72,* 371–377.

Allington, R. (1984). Content coverage and contextual reading in reading groups. *Journal of Reading Behavior, 16,* 85–96.

Allington, R. (1994). The schools we have. The schools we need. *The Reading Teacher, 48,* 14–29.

Almasi, J. (1995). The nature of fourth graders' sociocognitive conflicts in peer-led and teacher-led discussions of literature. *Reading Research Quarterly, 30,* 314–351.

Almasi, J. (1996). A new view of discussion. In L. Gambrell & J. Almasi (Eds.), *Lively discussions! Fostering engaged reading* (pp. 2–24). Newark, DE: International Reading Association.

Anderson, R. (1984). Role of the reader's schema in comprehension, learning, and memory. In R. Anderson, J. Osborn, and R. Tierney, (Eds.), *Learning to read in American schools: Basal readers and content texts.* Hillsdale, NJ: Erlbaum.

Anderson, R. C. (1996). Research foundations to support wide reading. In V. Creany (Ed.), *Promoting reading in developing countries* (pp. 55–77). Newark, DE: International Reading Association.

Anderson, R., Hiebert, E., Scott, J., & Wilkinson, I. (1985). *Becoming a nation of readers: The report of the Commission on Reading.* Washington, DC: The National Institute of Education, U.S. Department of Education.

Beck, I., McKeown, M., Hamilton, R., & Kucan, L. (1997). *Questioning the author: An approach for enhancing student engagement with text.* Newark, DE: International Reading Association.

Bird, L. (1988). Reading comprehension redefined through literature study: Creating worlds from the printed page. *The California Reader, 21,* 9–14.

Bloom, B. (1956). *Taxonomy of educational objectives: Handbook I, cognitive domain.* New York: David McKay.

Bloom, B. (1984). The search for methods of group instruction as effective as one-to-one tutoring. *Educational Leadership, 41*(8), 4–17.

Bracey, G. (1987). The social impact of ability grouping. *Phi Delta Kappan, 68,* 701–702.

Bransford, J. D., & McCarrell, N. S. (1974). A sketch of a cognitive approach to comprehension. In W. B. Weimer & D. S. Palermo (Eds.), *Cognition and the symbolic processes.* Hillsdale, NJ: Erlbaum.

Chomsky, C. (1972). Stages in language development and reading exposure. *Harvard Educational Review, 42,* 1–33.

Cohen, D. (1968). The effect of literature on vocabulary and reading achievement. *Elementary English, 45,* 209–213, 217.

Cummins, J. (1989). *Empowering minority students.* Sacramento: California Association for Bilingual Education.

Cunningham, A. E., & Stanovich, K. E. (1998). What reading does for the mind. *American Educator, 22,* 8–15.

DeFord, D. (1981). Literacy: Reading, writing, and other essentials. *Language Arts, 58,* 652–658.

DeFord, D. (1984). Classroom contexts for literacy learning. In T. Raphael (Ed.), *The context of school-based literacy* (pp. 163–180). New York: Random House.

Duke, N. (1999). *The scarcity of informational text in first grade.* University of Michigan-Ann Arbor: Center for the Improvement of Early Reading Achievement.

Durkin, D. (1979). What classroom observations reveal about reading comprehension instruction. *Reading Research Quarterly, 14,* 481–533.

Echevarria, J., & Graves, A. (1998). *Sheltered content instruction: Teaching English-language learners with diverse abilities.* Boston: Allyn and Bacon.

Eckhoff, B. (1983). How reading affects children's writing. *Language Arts, 60,* 607–616.

Edelsky, C. (1988). Living in the author's world: Analyzing the author's craft. *The California Reader, 21,* 9–14.

Eldredge, J., & Butterfield, D. (1986). Alternatives to traditional reading instruction. *The Reading Teacher, 40,* 32–37.

Feitelson, D., Kita, B., & Goldstein, Z. (1986). Effects of listening to series stories on first graders' comprehension and use of language. *Research in the Teaching of English, 20,* 339–355.

Fielding, L. G., & Pearson, P. D. (1994, February). Reading comprehension: What works. *Educational Leadership*, 62–68.

Foertsch, M. (1992). *Reading in and out of school. Factors influencing the literacy achievement of American students in grades 4, 8, and 12, in 1988 and 1990*. Washington, DC: Office of Educational Research and Improvement, U.S. Department of Education.

Gilles, C., Dickenson, J., McBride, C., & VanDover, M. (1994). Discussing our questions and questioning our discussions: Growing into literature study. *Language Arts, 71*, 499–508.

Hagerty, P., Hiebert, E., & Owens, M. (1989). Students' comprehension, writing, and perceptions in two approaches to literacy instruction. In S. McCormick and J. Zutell (Eds.), *Cognitive and social perspectives for literacy research and instruction* (pp. 453–459). Chicago: National Reading Conference.

Heller, M. (1991). *Reading-writing connections: From theory to practice*. New York: Longman.

Hiebert, E., & Colt, J. (1989). Patterns of literature-based reading instruction. *The Reading Teacher, 43*, 14–20.

Holdaway, D. (1979). *The foundations of literacy*. Exeter, NH: Heinemann.

Jewell, T., & Pratt, D. (1999). Literature discussions in the primary grades: Children's thoughtful discourse about books and what teachers can do to make it happen. *The Reading Teacher, 52* (8), 842–850.

Kagan, S. (1986). Cooperative learning and sociocultural factors in schooling. In *Beyond language: Social and cultural factors in schooling language minority students* (pp. 231–298). Los Angeles: Evaluation, Dissemination and Assessment Center, California State University.

Krashen, S. (1989). We acquire vocabulary and spelling by reading: Additional evidence for the input hypothesis. *The Modern Language Journal, 73*, 440–464.

Lancia, P. J. (1997). Literary borrowing: The effects of literature on children's writing. *The Reading Teacher, 50*, 470–475.

Langer, J. (1995) *Envisioning literature: Literary understanding and literature instruction*. New York: Teachers College Press.

Langer, J., Applebee, A., Mullis, I., & Foertsch, M. (1990). *Learning to read in our nation's schools: Instruction and achievement in 1988 at grades 4, 8, and 12. National Assessment of Educational Progress*. Princeton, NJ: Educational Testing Service.

Larrick, N. (1987). Illiteracy starts too soon. *Phi Delta Kappan, 69*, 184–189.

Morrow, L. M. (1992). The impact of a literature-based program on literacy achievement, use of literature, and attitudes of children from minority backgrounds. *Reading Research Quarterly, 27*, 250–275.

Morrow, L. M., O'Connor, E., and Smith, J. (1990). Effects of a story reading program on the literacy development of at risk kindergarten children. *Journal of Reading Behavior, 22*, 255–275.

Nagy, W., Herman, P., & Anderson, R. (1985). Learning words from context. *Reading Research Quarterly, 20*, 233–253.

O'Dell, S. (1960). *Island of the blue dolphins.* New York: Dell.

Purcell-Gates, V., McIntyre, E., & Freppon, P. A. (1995). Learning written storybook language in school: A comparison of low-SES children in skills-based and whole-language classroom. *American Educational Research Journal, 32*, 659–685.

Raphael, T. (2000). Balancing literature and instruction: Lessons from the Book Club Project. In B. Taylor, M. Graves, & P. van den Broek (Eds.), *Reading for meaning: Fostering comprehension in the middle grades* (pp. 70–94). New York: Teachers College Press.

Raphael, T., & McMahon, S. (1994). Book Club: An alternative framework for reading instruction. *The Reading Teacher, 48*, 102–116.

Rosenblatt, L. (1978). *The reader, the text, the poem.* Carbondale, IL: Southern Illinois University Press.

Rosenblatt, L. (1991). Literature—S.O.S.! *Language Arts, 68*, 444–448.

Scarcella, R., (1990). *Teaching language minority students in the multicultural classroom.* Englewood Cliffs, NJ: Prentice Hall.

Schifini, A. (1996). Discussion in multilingual, multicultural classrooms. In L. Gambrell & J. Almasi (Eds.), *Lively discussions! Fostering engaged reading* (pp. 39–49). Newark, DE: International Reading Association.

Shanahan, T. (1988). The reading-writing relationship: Seven instructional principles. *The Reading Teacher, 41*, 756–761.

Spangenberg-Urbschat, K., & Pritchard, R. (1994). *Kids come in all languages: Reading instruction for ESL students.* Newark, DE: International Reading Association.

Taylor, B. M., Pearson, P. D., Clark, K. F., & Walpole, S. (1999). *Beating the odds in teaching all children to read.* University of Michigan-Ann Arbor: Center for the Improvement of Early Reading Achievement.

Tunnell, M. & Jacobs, J. (1989). Using "real" books: Research findings on literature based reading instruction. *The Reading Teacher, 42*, 470–477.

van den Broek, P., & Kremer, K. (2000). The mind in action: What it means to comprehend during reading. In B. Taylor, M. Graves, & P. van den Broek (Eds.), *Reading for meaning: Fostering comprehension in the middle grades* (pp. 1–31). New York: Teachers College Press.

Walmsley, S., & Walp, T. (1989). *Teaching literature in elementary school.* Albany, NY: Center for the Learning and Teaching of Literature, University at Albany, State University of New York.

Wendler, D., Samuels, S. J., & Moore, V. (1989). The comprehension instruction of award-winning teachers, teachers with master's degrees, and other teachers. *Reading Research Quarterly, 24*, 382–401.

Wiencek, J., & O'Flahavan, J. (1994). From teacher-led to peer discussions about literature: Suggestions for making the shift. *Language Arts, 71*, 448–498.

Wuthrick, M. (1990). Blue jays win! Crows go down in defeat! *Phi Delta Kappan, 71*, 553–556.

Yopp, H. K., & Yopp, R. H. (1999). *Primary grade students' exposure to informational text.* Paper presented at the California Reading Association's annual conference research institute, Long Beach, CA, November 1999.

Yopp, R. H., & Yopp, H. K. (2000). Sharing informational text with young children. *The Reading Teacher, 53*, 410–429.

CHAPTER TWO

Prereading Activities

Prereading

Purposes	Activities
■ To promote personal responses	■ Anticipation guides
■ To activate and build background knowledge	■ Opinionnaires/ questionnaires
■ To set purposes for reading	■ Book boxes
■ To arouse curiosity and motivate students to read	■ Book bits
	■ Contrast charts
	■ Semantic maps
	■ KWL charts
	■ Preview-predict-confirm charts

The importance of engaging students in prereading activities cannot be overemphasized. Prereading activities promote personal responses to text by signaling students that their experiences, ideas, and thoughts matter. Prereading activities provide a forum for eliciting students' feelings and reactions to ideas and issues suggested by a reading selection before interacting with those ideas in the text. They prompt students to examine their own beliefs and promote students' understanding and appreciation of events in the book or decisions made by characters. Because they have thought about issues with which characters are confronted, students will identify more intensely with characters during reading.

In addition, it is through activities conducted prior to reading a selection that students can activate and build their background knowledge on topics or concepts addressed in the book. As discussed in Chapter One, activation of relevant knowledge is fundamental to comprehension. Because children may not spontaneously integrate what they read with what they know, special attention should be paid to preparation for reading. If relevant background knowledge cannot be assumed, knowledge-building activities should be provided. Finally, prereading activities serve to set purposes for reading, arouse students' curiosity, and motivate them to read.

In this chapter, we describe eight activities that may be used prior to reading a book, a chapter, or a passage. The first activity, the *anticipation guide*, prompts students to think about and take a stand on issues or ideas that they will later encounter. *Opinionnaires/questionnaires* are useful for tapping students' knowledge and previous related experiences as well as their beliefs and opinions on a subject. *Book boxes* and *book bits* provide students will clues about a selection. They serve to arouse curiosity and invite speculation about the characters, events, themes, or content of the book. *Contrast charts* are useful for helping students generate ideas in contrasting categories. *Semantic maps*, graphic depictions of categorical information, serve to build and activate background knowledge. *KWL charts* provide a simple format for students to identify what they know about a topic and what questions they have about the topic before reading about it. The *preview-predict-confirm* activity gives students the opportunity to preview texts in order to make predictions about their content. Each of these activities can serve to pique students' curiosity about a selection, prompting them to approach it with questioning minds.

Prereading activities are a critical part of the instructional cycle and should be used with the following purposes in mind:

- To invite students to respond personally to text by signalling them that their ideas, thoughts, and experiences matter
- To activate and build students' background knowledge on topics or concepts relevant to the book
- To set purposes for reading
- To arouse students' curiosity and motivate them to read

ANTICIPATION GUIDES

An anticipation guide (Readence, Bean, & Baldwin, 1981) is a list of statements with which the students are asked to agree or disagree. The statements are related to concepts, issues, or attitudes presented in the reading selection. Typically, three to six statements are used in an anticipation guide, and an effort is made to use statements that will result in differences of opinion and thus lead to discussion and debate.

The following steps may be used to develop and use an anticipation guide:

1. Identify major themes or ideas in the reading selection.
2. Write several statements related to selected themes or events that are likely to stimulate discussion.
3. Present the statements to the students on an overhead projector, on the chalkboard, or as a handout.
4. Allow a few minutes for students to respond privately to each statement by indicating their agreement or disagreement on paper.
5. Engage the students in a discussion about the statements by asking for their reactions. This discussion should include reasons for responses.

Asking students to take a stand on statements such as, "It's okay to disobey your parents," can generate lively discussion and prompt students to explore and identify their own attitudes and beliefs as well as to listen to the ideas of peers prior to interacting with the author's or a character's attitudes on the issue. The discussion might begin with the teacher or small-group student leader asking for a show of hands on the first statement, "How many of you agree with this statement?" "How many of you disagree?" Then the teacher or leader should ask students to share their reasons. Students should be provided opportunities to respond to their peers' comments. This format may be followed with each of the statements. The discussions that ensue are typically quite revealing about students' attitudes and background knowledge. Thus, they provide the teacher with information that may influence instructional decisions.

Sample anticipation guides for several books are presented on the next few pages. A brief summary of each book is provided for the teacher and is not intended to be shared with the students. Actual student responses are offered in italics for one of the examples. It is important that the teacher remember that we are not suggesting that these are "correct" responses. They are provided here so the teacher can more fully understand the activity. Student responses will, and should, vary.

Example 2.1 _____

- **Title:** *Fly Away Home*
- **Author:** Eve Bunting

- **Grade Level:** K–3
- **Summary:** A homeless young boy and his father live in the airport and move from location to location in order to avoid being noticed.

Anticipation Guide

Agree	Disagree	
_____	_____	1. All people live in houses or apartments.
_____	_____	2. It would be easy to hide in an airport.
_____	_____	3. It is sad when people around you don't notice you.

Example 2.2 _____

- **Title:** *Teammates*
- **Author:** Peter Golenbock
- **Grade Level:** 1–4
- **Summary:** This book describes the prejudice experienced by Jackie Robinson, the first black player in Major League baseball. It highlights his courage and the support he received from Pee Wee Reese, a white teammate.

Anticipation Guide

Agree	Disagree	
_____	_____	1. Staying away from people who are cruel to you is a good idea.
_____	_____	2. It's fun to be different.
_____	_____	3. When you are very good at something, people like you.
_____	_____	4. Sometimes one person can make a difference in the world.
_____	_____	5. If everybody is being cruel to someone, there's probably a good reason.

Example 2.3 _____

- **Title:** *The Book of the Pig*
- **Author:** Jack Denton Scott
- **Grade Level:** 4–6
- **Summary:** This book dispels many myths about pigs and provides much information about their activities, the variety of breeds, and the many ways they serve people.

Anticipation Guide

Agree	Disagree	
_____	_____	1. Pigs are dirty animals.
_____	_____	2. Pigs serve no useful purpose.
_____	_____	3. Pigs are affectionate animals.
_____	_____	4. Pigs are stupid animals.
_____	_____	5. Pigs can be trained to do tricks.
_____	_____	6. Pigs are fussy about what they eat.

Example 2.4 _____

- **Title:** *Flying Solo*
- **Author:** Ralph Fletcher
- **Grade Level:** 4–8
- **Summary:** The students in Mr. Fabiano's sixth-grade class decide not to report that the substitute has failed to show up. The students, including Rachel, who has been mute since a classmate's death, and Bastion, who is struggling with an impending move, learn much about themselves and one another during the day.

Anticipation Guide

Agree	Disagree	
_____	_____	1. Students are capable of running a class without a teacher.
_____	_____	2. You should try to avoid thinking about things that bother you.

_____	_____	3. It is important to do what is best for you, even if it is not good for someone else.
_____	_____	4. On important decisions, the majority should rule.

Example 2.5 _____

- **Title:** *Tuck Everlasting*
- **Author:** Natalie Babbitt
- **Grade Level:** 4–8
- **Summary:** Ten-year-old Winnie Foster stumbles upon the Tuck family's secret: that they will live forever. Those who drink from a particular spring in a wood near the Foster's home—which the Tucks did inadvertantly 87 years ago—cannot die. Is eternal life a blessing or a curse? The Tuck family briefly kidnaps Winnie in order to convince her to keep the secret, but a strange man, too, has learned the secret. His goal is to take possession of the spring and make a fortune selling the water. In this thought-provoking story, Winnie faces a number of moral dilemmas and ultimately accomplishes something she always hoped: to do something important for the world.

Anticipation Guide

Agree	**Disagree**	
_____	_____	1. It would be wonderful to live forever.
_____	_____	2. You should never do something that your parents have forbidden.
_____	_____	3. Some secrets are so important that it is acceptable to do anything in order to keep them.
_____	_____	4. People should have the right to sell products even if they are harmful.
_____	_____	5. It is OK to hurt one person to protect many.

In addition to indicating their agreement or disagreement with statements in an anticipation guide, students may be asked to write a brief comment in response to each statement, as in Example 2.6.

Example 2.6

- **Title:** *Dragonwings*
- **Author:** Laurence Yep
- **Grade Level:** 5–8
- **Summary:** An eight-year-old boy travels from China to the United States to be with his father whom he has never seen. There he confronts prejudice and discrimination as well as his own misperceptions about Americans. He watches his father struggle toward achieving his dream to fly. The story takes place in the early 1900s and was inspired by the actual account of a Chinese immigrant who built a flying machine in 1909.

Anticipation Guide

Agree	Disagree	
X		1. It would be exciting to move to a new country. *I think you'd see a lot of interesting things in another country.*
	X	2. Discrimination and prejudice often work both ways between immigrants and native peoples. *Usually the people already living in a country don't like newcomers, but newcomers want to be friends.*
	X	3. A father has a duty to always protect his children from harm. *Parents should take care of their children, but eventually children must take care of themselves.*
X		4. People should not spend energy working on unrealistic goals. *If it's unrealistic, it's stupid for someone to spend time on it. He should find another goal.*

The anticipation guide shown in Example 2.6 was presented to graduate students before its purpose or its relationship to a piece of literature was explained. What ensued was a thoughtful and lengthy discussion. The participants thought about the ideas, related them to their own experiences, shared interpretations of and responses to the statements, and supported their viewpoints.

Completed anticipation guides may be saved for reconsideration after a selection has been read. The format of the anticipation guide can be easily changed to include a single column for anticipation responses in which students put a plus or a minus symbol (or a smiling or frowning face) indicating agreement or disagreement, and a second column for reaction responses. Students complete this second column after reading the selection.

Upon completing the activity the second time, students may discover that their attitudes and understandings have changed as a result of their reading. Such changes are intriguing to students and may be a stimulus for writing.

OPINIONNAIRES/QUESTIONNAIRES

Opinionnaires/questionnaires (Reasoner, 1976) are useful tools for helping readers examine their own values, attitudes, opinions, or related experiences before they read the book. Constructing an opinionnaire/questionnaire is very much like constructing an anticipation guide. The teacher first identifies themes, ideas, or major events around which he or she wishes to focus his or her instruction. Then he or she generates a series of questions to tap students' opinions, attitudes, or past experiences related to those themes. Some items on the opinionnaires/questionnaires may be open-ended, whereas others may be more structured and offer students a checklist of possible responses.

Keep in mind that the purpose of this activity is to facilitate students' thinking about their own attitudes and experiences related to selected issues, not to elicit "correct" responses. Be accepting of students' honest responses and do not do what one student teacher we observed did. He continued to probe a student who made a comment apparently contrary to his own values until she finally changed her response. The student grew increasingly uncomfortable and it became obvious to the entire class that the student teacher was trying to elicit a particular response. He was not truly interested in his students' opinions. Needless to say, the student teacher's behavior served as a roadblock to the grand conversation that the activity could have prompted.

The opinionnaire/questionnaire depicted in Example 2.7 provides a structure for students to talk about bullies. When they subsequently hear or read the story *The Bully of Barkham Street*, they are more likely to appreciate the story events. Note that extra spaces are included so that students may insert their own ideas.

Example 2.7 _____

- **Title:** *The Bully of Barkham Street*
- **Author:** Mary Stolz
- **Grade Level:** 4–6
- **Summary:** Martin Hastings is a neighborhood bully who has few friends. He emerges as a sympathetic character who begins to make efforts to change his reputation.

Opinionnaire/Questionnaire

1. What words best describe a bully?

_____ heroic	_____ wise guy	_____ mean
_____ conceited	_____ unloved	_____ spoiled
_____ babyish	_____ poor	_____ wealthy
_____ _____	_____ _____	_____ _____

2. What do you think causes a person to become a bully?

   _____ He's just born that way.

   _____ Too many people have picked on him and made him mean.

   _____ He's a bully so he can get attention.

   _____ He thinks he's uglier than most people his age.

   _____ He's bigger than most people his age.

   _____ He's smaller than most people his age.

3. How would you recognize a bully?

   _____ From the way he brags

   _____ From the expression on his face

   _____ From the way he walks

   _____ From the way he talks

_____ From the way he teases people

_____ _____

_____ _____

4. How would you cure a bully?

     _____ With love and kindness

     _____ With strict rules and punishment

     _____ By giving him a taste of his own medicine

     _____ By getting a meaner bully to frighten him

     _____ _____

     _____ _____

Note: This example was condensed from Reasoner (1972).

Reasoner (1972) suggested that students use the opinionnaire/ questionnaire to poll others (students in other classrooms, parents, etc.) to see what they believe. The data may then be compiled for class summary and evaluation.

Example 2.8 _____

- ■ **Title:** *Roll of Thunder, Hear My Cry*
- ■ **Author:** Mildred Taylor
- ■ **Grade Level:** 6–8
- ■ **Summary:** Set in the south during the Depression, this story relates the struggles of a black family and its encounters with hate and prejudice.

Opinionnaire/Questionnaire

Listed below are a few incidents that make some people feel bad. Which of them would make you feel bad?

_____ When someone you love is ashamed of you

_____ When people call you names

_____ When people act as if they are better than you

_____ When you are punished for something you did that you should not have done

_____ When someone stares at you

_____ _____

_____ _____

_____ _____

What would you do if you were tricked out of a favorite possession by someone you knew?

_____ Cry.

_____ Tell your parents and ask for their help.

_____ Tell that person's parents and ask for their help.

_____ Tell all your friends so they won't be nice to that person.

_____ Get it back somehow.

_____ Pretend you didn't like the possession anyway.

_____ Decide you didn't deserve the possession.

_____ Trick that person out of something to show him or her how it feels.

_____ _____

_____ _____

If you were in a store and the clerk who was waiting on you stopped helping you and turned to assist two other people, what would you do?

_____ Wait patiently.

_____ Leave and go somewhere else.

_____ Leave and tell your parents.

_____ Complain to the manager.

_____ Demand that the clerk finish helping you.

_____ _____

A boy in your class is always bothering you, acting smarter than you, and getting into mischief. Which of the following describe what you would do?

_____ Feel sorry for him.

_____ Try to be his friend and help him change.

_____ Ignore him.

_____ Beat him up.

_____ Hope someone catches him someday.

_____ Tell on him.

_____ _____

_____ _____

If he came to you for help, what would you do?

_____ Tell him "No way!"

_____ Help him.

_____ Laugh at him.

_____ Pretend you'd help him, then don't.

_____ _____

_____ _____

As with the anticipation guides, opinionnaires/questionnaires may be distributed again after students have read the book. Students may examine whether their reponses have changed, and if so, why they have changed.

BOOK BOXES

The book box activity stimulates thinking about a selection before reading it. In this activity, students are provided with clues and encouraged to make predictions about the content of the selection.

If you are going to share a book with the whole class, begin by telling students that they soon will be reading a new book and that you have some objects in a book box that are somehow related to the selection. If your students will be working in small groups, provide each group with a book box related to the book the students are reading.

In either case, let your students know that each object in the box provides some information about the selection and that their job is to think about what the object tells them about the selection. One item is drawn from the box at a time. Students should identify the object; this is particularly important when unusual or unfamiliar objects are included in the box. After the first object is shared, some time should be spent discussing the object and its possible relevance. Then, a second item is drawn from the box and discussion continues. As each new item is drawn from the box, students' predictions about the selection are revised. Repeat this process until each of the objects has been drawn from the box.

It is important that students are given ample time to talk with one another and to share their visions and revisions of the selection. Hearing the experiences, knowledge, and thinking processes of peers supports students' own understandings.

When we have used this activity, we notice that students are highly engaged as they read the selection. They are alert for the author's usage of each of the objects and intrigued by how well they did or did not predict the role each of the objects plays in the text.

Example 2.9 _____

- **Title:** *The First Strawberries*
- **Author:** Joseph Bruchac
- **Grade Level:** K–3
- **Summary:** This Cherokee legend tells the origin of strawberries on earth. A woman, angry at her husband for his harsh words when she is picking flowers rather than cooking their

meal, walks away from him. He follows her but cannot catch up to her. The sun chooses to help the man because he is sorry for his words. Shining on the earth, the sun causes raspberries to grow in front of the woman as she walks. She does not stop. The sun beams down on the earth again and blueberries and blackberries grow. Still the woman does not stop. Trying its hardest, the sun shines on the grass and strawberries appear. The strawberries look so appealing that the woman stops to eat a few. Their sweetness remind her of the happiness she had shared with her husband and she remains to gather more. Her husband catches up to her and asks her forgiveness. She responds by sharing the sweet fruit.

Objects in the Book Box

figurines of a husband and wife (wedding attire makes this relationship explicit)

a bunch of flowers

some strawberries

Example 2.10

- **Title:** *Holes*
- **Author:** Louis Sachar
- **Grade Level:** 4–8
- **Summary:** When given the choice between Camp Green Lake (a detention center) and traditional prison, the family of Stanley Yelnats sends him to Camp Green Lake to serve a sentence for a crime he did not commit. Camp Green Lake is never green, nor does it have a lake; it is a barren wasteland in the middle of Texas. Boys serving their terms there must dig a five-foot-deep hole in the dry hard dirt every day, ostensibly to build character, but in truth because the warden hopes to uncover a treasure left by a notorious bandit a century ago. Bad fortune has followed Stanley and his forebears for generations. This eventful and sometime humorous tale that weaves the past with the present is a Newbery Medal book.

(continued)

Objects in the Book Box

shovel	sneakers
onion	jar of peaches
handcuffs, sheriff's badge, or some item to represent the law	tube of lipstick
	small container of sand

Book boxes can be a springboard for writing. After students discuss the objects and make predictions about the selection they are to read, they might independently do a quickwrite, developing a narrative that makes sense of and connects the objects or an expository piece that explains the relationship among the items. Also, the students might develop a chart that lists participants' hypotheses about the setting, characters, and events (for narratives) or setting, topics, and information (for expository text). The same set of objects might lead students in very different directions and result in two group charts, one for narrative and one for expository text.

Example 2.11 provides additional book box suggestions.

Example 2.11 _____

Book	Author	Grade	Objects in the Book Box
Bunny Cakes	Rosemary Wells	K–2	mixing bowl candles piece of paper with scribbles on it mud (in a container)
Cloudy with a Chance of Meatballs	Judi Barrett	K–2	plate box of pancake mix clippings from the newspaper of the weather report umbrella

			package of spaghetti slices of bread small boat
Bananas!	Jacqueline Farmer	2–5	banana magnifying glass fork twine plastic bag apple

BOOK BITS

Book bits are similar to book boxes in that bits of information are shared with students before they read. Instead of sharing objects, however, sentences or phrases from the text are shared. Interacting with these brief quotes piques students' curiosity and stimulates thinking about the text. In order to use this strategy the teacher selects a number of sentences or phrases from throughout the text and writes each on a small strip of paper. There should be as many quotes as there are students in the group so everyone can participate—and they should be quotes that are significant to the text. These "book bits" should reveal enough to help students begin to think along the lines that support text understanding, but not so revealing that they limit thinking.

Each student takes a book bit, reads it, and reflects on it for a moment. Students think to themselves about what impression they are beginning to form about the text. Then students move around the room and read their book bits to one another. No discussion occurs during this sharing, only the reading of the book bits. Once students have had the opportunity to hear most of their peers' book bits, they might do a quickwrite on impressions they now have. What is the selection about? What do we know about any characters? What do we think will happen, or what have we learned about the topic? After a few moments, students discuss their ideas with one another.

If sentences are selected carefully, students will form a number of plausible impressions and predictions. If the sentences have revealed too much, the students' responses will converge.

Example 2.12 _____

- **Title:** *Fireflies!*
- **Author:** Julie Brinckloe
- **Grade Level:** K–3
- **Summary:** A young boy and his friends capture fireflies in glass jars and are delighted to watch them glow. As the light in the jar begins to dim, the boy tearfully realizes that he should set his fireflies free or they will die.

Book Bits
(for a group of seven students)

It was growing dark.
Something flickered there.
I poked holes in the top of the jar with Momma's scissors.
We ran like crazy.
I shut my eyes tight and put the pillow of over my head.
The jar glowed like moonlight.
"Catch them, catch them!" we cried.

Notice that in Example 2.12, the word "fireflies" does not appear in any of the book bits. This was a deliberate decision on the part of the teacher. Had the word "fireflies" appeared in a book bit (or had the teacher revealed the title of the book), students' thinking would have narrowed very quickly and their opportunities to build interpretations would have been limited. Instead, students form a variety of impressions as they read their own strips. As they gather information from their peers, they may experience cognitive conflict. Their initial impressions may have to be abandoned in favor of new interpretations that better account for additional information, and their interpretations continue to be revised as they obtain more and more information from their peers.

Example 2.13 _____

- **Title:** *The Great Gilly Hopkins*
- **Author:** Katherine Paterson
- **Grade Level:** 4–8

■ **Summary:** Gilly Hopkins has bounced from one foster home to another and has not allowed herself to love anyone. The eleven-year-old is bright, tough, and defiant. Gilly begins to soften under the care of Maime Trotter and, although she fights it, she cannot stop herself from growing fond of Trotter's other foster child, William Earnest, and their blind neighbor, Mr. Randolph.

Book Bits
(for a class of eighteen students)

"This will be your third home in less than three years."

"Will you do me a favor, Gilly? Try to get off on the right foot?"

Gilly carefully spread the gum under the handle of the left-hand door as a sticky surprise for the next person who might try to open it.

She turned her back on them. That would show them.

Oh, why did it have to be so hard? Other kids could be with their mothers all the time.

I don't need help from anybody.

"That was Mr. Randolph. He can't see a thing. You've got to go back and bring him by the hand, so he won't fall."

They continued to read that way. He would listen blissfully for a while and then join, turning her single voice into the sound of a choir.

"She's a handsome reader, all right."

It was only a matter of getting back into Mr. Randolph's house and getting the rest of the money. There was sure to be more.

She wasn't going to let a bunch of low-class idiots think they were smarter than she was.

The look on Trotter's face was the one Gilly had, in some deep part of her, longed to see all her life, but not from someone like Trotter.

"You and I are two of the angriest people I know."

Her heart was pumping crazily. She made herself sit down.

People were so dumb sometimes you almost felt bad to take advantage of them—but not too bad.

If she didn't watch herself, she'd start liking the little jerk.

(continued)

She was not going to panic. He couldn't see. Of course, he couldn't see.

She had known that it never pays to attach yourself to something that is likely to blow away.

CONTRAST CHARTS

Contrast charts also may be used to facilitate students' thinking about ideas prior to encountering them in a story. They are very simple to develop, requiring only that the teacher identify theme-related contrasting categories under which students can list ideas. For example, in the book *Island of the Blue Dolphins*, by Scott O'Dell, Karana is left alone on an island for years and must learn to deal with loneliness. To tap students' feelings about and experiences with loneliness before they encounter Karana's feelings, the teacher might ask students to generate a list of times when they feel lonely and times when they do not feel lonely.

Contrast charts may be generated by the class as a whole, by small groups of children, or by individuals. We encourage the use of small groups with this activity. One student records the ideas of the group, then each group shares its ideas with classmates.

Example 2.14 _____

- **Title:** *Frog and Toad Are Friends*
- **Author:** Arnold Lobel
- **Grade Level:** K–2
- **Summary:** Frog and Toad, the best of friends, have many adventures together.

Contrast Chart

Some people are good to have as friends and some people aren't. List some of the qualities that are important to you in a good friend. Then list qualities that make a person a bad friend.

Good Friend	Bad Friend
1. *shares with you*	1. *tells your secrets to others*
2. *is nice*	2. *doesn't share*

3. *gives you things*
4.
5.
6.

3. *won't play with you*
4.
5.
6.

Example 2.15 _____

- **Title:** *Alexander and the Terrible, Horrible, No Good, Very Bad Day*
- **Author:** Judith Viorst
- **Grade Level:** K–3
- **Summary:** Alexander has a horrible day when one thing after another goes wrong for him.

Contrast Chart

Have you ever heard people say, "That made my day!" or "That ruined my day"? They are referring to events that happened that make them feel especially good or particularly miserable and cranky. List some things that could happen to you that could make your day either good or bad.

Good Day	Bad Day
1.	1.
2.	2.
3.	3.
4.	4.
5.	5.
6.	6.

Students easily generate ideas for the chart in Example 2.15. They then are quite sympathetic with Alexander's misadventures and usually become very excited if Alexander confronts one of the very events that they listed as making their own day a bad one.

In Example 2.16 children respond to the idea of moving. This move could be from one country to another (as the character experiences), one house to another, or one classroom to another. By asking children to think about the positive and negative aspects of moving, teachers are setting the stage for students to understand the character's mixed feelings of joy and loss.

Example 2.16

- **Title:** *Grandfather's Journey*
- **Author:** Allen Say
- **Grade Level:** 1–3
- **Summary:** A Japanese-American man tells the story of his grandfather's move to America and of his feelings of love and longing for both his native country and his adopted country.

Contrast Chart

Good Things about Moving	Bad Things about Moving
1.	1.
2.	2.
3.	3.
4.	4.
5.	5.
6.	6.

Example 2.17

- **Title:** *Stuart Little*
- **Author:** E. B. White
- **Grade Level:** 4–6
- **Summary:** This story tells the humorous adventures of a two-inch mouse who is born into a human family.

Contrast Chart

What would it be like if you were two inches tall? List some things that would be difficult to do. List some things that would be easy to do.

Difficult	Easy
1.	1.
2.	2.
3.	3.
4.	4.
5.	5.
6.	6.

Children find this book very entertaining. They are amused as Stuart's size becomes advantageous at certain times and quite a problem at others. Some of the incidents the students are sure not to anticipate!

SEMANTIC MAPS

Semantic maps are graphic displays of categorized information. They may be used to build vocabulary and to activate and organize students' background knowledge on a given topic (Johnson & Pearson, 1984; Johnson, Pittelman, & Heimlich, 1986). They give students anchor points to which new concepts they will encounter can be attached (McNeil, 1987). To make a semantic map, the teacher first writes and encircles a term that is central to the reading selection on the chalkboard. In a selection about schools, for example, the teacher might write the word "school" in the middle of the chalkboard. He or she next generates categories related to the central concept. For our school example, he or she might write "rooms," "people," and "studies." Each is encircled and lines are drawn from the categories to the central concept of "school" to indicate a relationship. Then the teacher elicits from the students exemplars, details, or subordinate ideas for each of the categories. Within the category of "people," for example, the students may list "children," "teachers," "principal," and so on. These terms are written in the category circles. The teacher leads the students in a discussion about the terms and their relationships. Research suggests that this discussion is key to the effectiveness of the technique (Stahl & Vancil, 1986). Once a map is generated, the class may want to save it to refer to during or after reading. At any point the map may be modified to reflect new information or ideas.

Another way to develop a semantic map is to have the students brainstorm and record the subordinate ideas after being told the central concept and then to group them into categories and label the categories. This approach is similar to Taba's (1967) list-group-label technique for concept development.

The use of semantic maps prior to reading has been found to result in better story recall in low-ability readers than the use of the more traditional directed reading technique in which new content, new vocabulary, and the purpose for reading a selection are discussed prior to reading (Sinatra, Stahl-Gemake, & Berg, 1984). The use of semantic maps is supported by schema theory described in Chapter One. Schemata (plural of schema) are networks of knowledge that readers' store in their minds. Semantic maps help students tap those networks, integrate new information, and restructure existing networks.

Example 2.18 _____

- **Title:** *Peppe the Lamplighter*
- **Author:** Elisa Bartone
- **Grade Level:** K–3
- **Summary:** Young Peppe wants to help support his family and accepts a job as the lamplighter in Little Italy, a New York City neighborhood. His father, initially upset about Peppe's choice of work, ultimately is proud of his son.

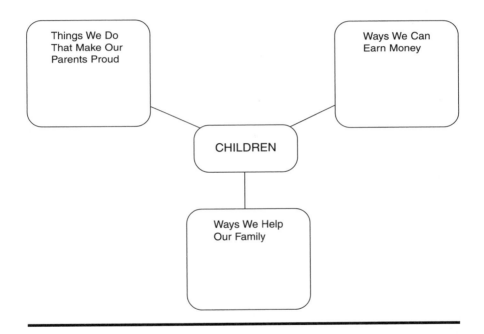

Example 2.19 _____

- **Title:** *In the Year of the Boar and Jackie Robinson*
- **Author:** Bette Lord
- **Grade Level:** 4–6
- **Summary:** This book tells the story of an immigrant family's experiences in the United States.

(continued)

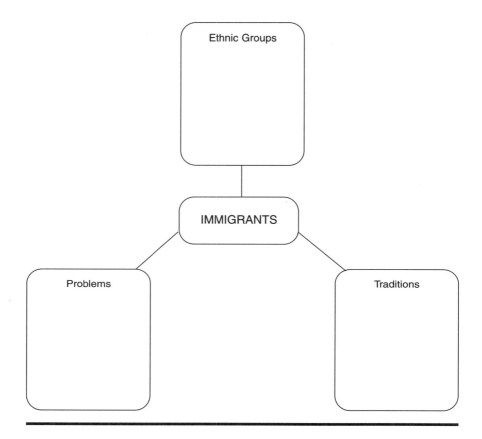

KWL CHARTS

Another activity that helps students access their background knowledge on a given subject is the KWL (know, want to know, learned) chart developed by Ogle (1986). The KWL chart is intended to be used before and then after reading or listening to a selection that contains some factual content. Prior to interacting with the selection, the students brainstorm and write on a chart all they know about a given topic. In a second column, students record what they would like to know about the topic. For example, prior to reading the poem "Honeybees" in *Joyful Noise*, by Paul Fleischman, students would record everything they know about honeybees in one column and what they want to know in a second column, as in Example 2.20. By identifying questions, students develop their reasons for reading, and as a result are more likely to be actively engaged in the reading process.

Example 2.20

- **Title:** "Honeybees" from *Joyful Noise*
- **Author:** Paul Fleischman
- **Grade Level:** K–6
- **Summary:** This poem, one of a collection of poems about insects, describes the activities of the queen and worker honeybees.

KWL Chart
Honeybees

What we know	What we want to know
make honey	*How is the queen different?*
live in hives	*Who lays the eggs?*
have a queen	*How many are laid at a time?*
sting	*How far away do bees fly from their hives?*
	Why does the sting hurt so much?

Once the selection has been read, students record in a third column what they have learned about the topic as a result of having read the selection. In addition, any information listed in the first column that was inaccurate is noted.

Example 2.21

- **Title:** *It's an Ant's Life*
- **Author:** Ant, with help from Steve Parker
- **Grade Level:** 3–5
- **Summary:** In this first-person journal, the author (an ant!) provides a wealth of information about ants. The journal makes use of diagrams, clippings, maps, and a glossary of "more than ten important words."

(continued)

KWL Chart
Ants

What we know	**What we want to know**	**What we learned**

It is important that the teacher restrict use of this activity to books that contain accurate information. Do not ask students what they know and what they have learned about whales from a work of fiction that presents whales that chat with one another and have cute personalities. The wonderful story of *Gilberto and the Wind*, by Marie Hall Ets, anthropomorphizes the wind, using phrases such as "Wind likes my soap bubbles" and "Wind is all tired out" that clearly are inappropriate to include on a KWL chart. Therefore, the activity should not be used with this particular book.

By no means, however, should this activity be restricted to use with nonfiction. Many works of fiction have considerable content that students often do not realize they are learning. In *Johnny Tremain*, by Esther Forbes, students learn a great deal about the Revolutionary War. In *Where the Red Fern Grows*, by Wilson Rawls, students learn about life in the Ozarks. In *Miracles on Maple Hill*, by Virginia Sorensen, students learn about the production of maple syrup. The teacher must be familiar with the reading selection and be confident that information presented about a topic under consideration is accurate before using it in a KWL chart.

It is likely that a number of questions generated by the students will not be addressed by the reading selection. Students should be encouraged to pursue other sources of information. Ogle (1986) says that this helps students recognize the "priority of their personal desire to learn over simply taking in what the author has chosen to include" (p. 567). She suggests adding a fourth column (KWLH) in which students suggest how they will obtain the information (D. Ogle, personal communication, December 2, 1994).

An additional modification of this versatile chart includes a column on affect (KWLA) to be completed after reading (Mandeville, 1994). Students may use this column to respond personally to the information they have learned, indicating what they find most interesting in the selection, identifying parts in the reading they liked the best or least, or noting why some information is particularly important to them. This linking of affective and cognitive domains has tremendous potential to spark students' interest in the factual information presented in many books, and Mandeville suggests that students who attach their own importance and personal relevance to information are likely to comprehend and remember the information better.

PREVIEW-PREDICT-CONFIRM CHARTS

In the preview-predict-confirm activity, students have the opportunity to quickly preview a book before making predictions about its content. Each student has a copy of the book and spends a few moments looking through it. Then books are closed and students, as a group, generate a list of words they anticipate will appear in the text, offering explanations for their predictions. For instance, in Example 2.22 one child indicated that he thought the word "Texas" would be in the selection because he knows cowboys live in Texas. Another child explained her contribution of the word "desert" by stating that the pictures show the cowboys and cattle in the desert. A third child explained his prediction of the words "bandanna" and "boots" by stating that he saw a diagram of cowboys' clothing.

Once the students have previewed and predicted, they read (or listen to) the book. After reading, they review their list, noting and discussing which predictions were confirmed.

This activity elicits vocabulary related to the book, activates and builds background knowledge, encourages active engagement through predictions, and provides a window on the thinking strategies of peers. Further, children experience a sense of satisfaction when they see the author use the words they predicted, and the activity heightens students' awareness of the value of previewing. Finally, this activity gives the teacher some information about how close a match exists between the language and content of the text and the language and background knowledge of the students.

Example 2.22 _____

- **Title** *Yippee-Yay!*
- **Author:** Gail Gibbons
- **Grade:** 2–5
- **Summary:** In this text, Gibbons provides interesting information about cowboy life in the Old West.

Preview-Predict-Confirm Chart

Word Predictions	Appeared in Text?	
	Yes	**No**
cowboy	x	
horse	x	
clothes	x	
hat	x	
boots	x	
cattle	x	
bronco	x	
trails	x	
map		x
rope	x	
brands	x	
songs	x	
towns	x	
desert		x
hot		x
Texas	*x (on map)*	
bandanna	x	
campfire	x	

CONCLUSION

The eight prereading activities described in this chapter set the stage for personal responses to the literature, activate or build background knowledge, help students think about their beliefs and attitudes related to issues in a reading selection, and motivate students to read. Anticipation guides, opinionnaires/questionnaires, book boxes, book bits, contrast charts, semantic maps, KWL charts, and preview-predict-confirm charts involve students in thinking, discussing, responding, exploring, and shaping ideas.

It is hoped that the students will find the literature personally meaningful after engaging in these activities and that they will approach ideas contained in the books with greater interest, purpose, involvement, and appreciation.

REFERENCES

Babbitt, N. (1975). *Tuck everlasting*. New York: Farrar, Straus & Giroux.
Barrett, J. (1985). *Cloudy with a chance of meatballs*. New York: Life Oak Media.
Bartone, E. (1993). *Peppe the lamplighter*. New York: Lothrop, Lee & Shepard.
Brinckloe, J. (1985). *Fireflies!* New York: Aladdin.
Bruchac, J. (1993). *The first strawberries*. New York: Penguin Puffin.
Bunting, E. (1991). *Fly away home*. New York: Clarion.
Ets, M. H. (1963). *Gilberto and the wind*. New York: Scholastic.
Farmer, J. (1999). *Bananas!* Watertown, MA: Charlesbridge.
Fleischman, P. (1988). *Joyful noise*. New York: HarperTrophy.
Fletcher, R. (1998). *Flying solo*. New York: Clarion.
Forbes, E. (1971). *Johnny Tremain*. New York: Dell.
Gibbons, G. (1998). *Yippee-yay!* New York: Little, Brown.
Golenbock, P. (1990). *Teammates*. San Diego, CA: Harcourt Brace.
Hall, D. (1979). *Ox-cart man*. New York: Penguin.
Johnson, D. J. & Pearson, P. D. (1984). *Teaching reading vocabulary* (2nd ed.). New York: Holt, Rinehart, & Winston.
Johnson, D., Pittelman, S., & Heimlich, J. (1986). Semantic mapping. *The Reading Teacher, 39*, 778–783.
Lobel, A. (1970). *Frog and toad are friends*. New York: Scholastic.
Lord, B. (1984). *In the year of the boar and Jackie Robinson*. New York: Harper Junior Books.
Mandeville, T. F. (1994). KWLA: Linking the affective and cognitive domains. *The Reading Teacher, 47*, 679–680.
McNeil, J. (1987). *Reading comprehension: New directions for classroom practice* (2nd ed.). Glenview, IL: Scott, Foresman.
O'Dell, S. (1960). *Island of the blue dolphins*. New York: Houghton Mifflin.
Ogle, D. (1986). K-W-L: A teaching model that develops active reading of expository text. *The Reading Teacher, 39*, 564–570.
Parker, S. (1999). *It's an ant's life*. Pleasantville, NY: Reader's Digest Children's Books.
Paterson, K. *The great Gilly Hopkins*. New York: HarperTrophy.
Rawls, W. (1961). *Where the red fern grows*. New York: Doubleday.
Readence, J., Bean, T., & Baldwin, R. (1981). *Content area reading: An integrated approach*. Dubuque, IA: Kendall/Hunt.
Reasoner, C.F. (1972). *Where the readers are*. New York: Dell.
Reasoner, C. F. (1976). *Releasing children to literature* (revised ed.). New York: Dell.

Sachar, L. (1998). *Holes*. New York: Farrar, Straus & Giroux.

Say, A. (1993). *Grandfather's journey*. Boston: Houghton Mifflin.

Scott, J. D. (1981). *The book of the pig*. New York: G. P. Putnam's Sons.

Sinatra, R., Stahl-Gemake, J., & Berg, D. (1984). Improving reading comprehension of disabled readers through semantic mapping. *The Reading Teacher, 38*, 22–29.

Sorensen, V. (1957). *Miracles on Maple Hill*. New York: Harcourt Brace & World.

Stahl, S., & Vancil, S. (1986). Discussion is what makes semantic maps work in vocabulary instruction. *The Reading Teacher, 40*, 62–67.

Stolz, M. (1977). *The bully of Barkham Street*. New York: Dell.

Taba, H. (1967). *Teachers handbook for elementary social studies*. Reading, MA: Addison-Wesley.

Taylor, M. (1983). *Roll of thunder, hear my cry*. Toronto: Bantam.

Viorst, J. (1972). *Alexander and the terrible, horrible, no good, very bad day*. New York: Atheneum.

Wells, R. (1997). *Bunny cakes*. New York: Dial.

White, E. B. (1973). *Stuart Little*. New York: Harper & Row.

Yep, L. (1975). *Dragonwings*. New York: Harper Junior Books.

CHAPTER THREE

During-Reading Activities

During Reading

Purposes

- To facilitate comprehension
- To focus attention
- To encourage reactions to ideas
- To call attention to language
- To allow for personal responses

Activities

- Literature circles
- Literature maps
- Character maps
- Character webs
- Character perspective charts
- Journals
- Feelings charts
- Contrast charts

Although there will be many occasions when teachers will wish to introduce a book and then let the children read it uninterrupted, during some literature experiences, they will want to provide activities that enhance students' understanding of the selection or focus their attention on particular themes, issues, characters, or events. Furthermore, teachers will want to provide activities that prompt students to react to ideas, events, or characters or to identify what they find interesting or meaningful. In other words, they will want to enhance the interactions between the students and the text.

Rosenblatt (1978) referred to these interactions between readers and texts as *transactions* in order to emphasize the dynamic relationship between the two. She argued that readers infuse intellectual and emotional meanings into the patterns of symbols we call words and that "the special meanings and associations that words in a book have for each reader will determine what the work communicates to him [or her]" (p. 25). She stated that an important task for the teacher is to foster fruitful transactions between the reader and the text. One way to do this is to provide an environment in which students are allowed to respond personally to works of literature and to explore and compare their responses to those of classmates.

The activities presented in this chapter, indeed in this book, provide these opportunities. Students are encouraged to bring themselves to the literary experience and respond personally to the text. They are encouraged to listen to the points of view of others and are given opportunities to reflect on and analyze their own responses. In addition, some of these activities are excellent tools for calling students' attention to effective use of language. One of the advantages of using literature in the classroom is that it provides a rich language model.

This chapter describes eight activities in which teachers may engage children during reading. *Literature circles* encourage students to respond to a text in a variety of ways. *Literature maps* enhance students' comprehension by assisting them in identifying and organizing information they find important or interesting. Literature maps can be used to focus students' attention on text elements, such as setting and characters; to call attention to language; and to allow for personal responses. *Character maps* are used specifically for analyzing characters and their evolving relationships. *Character webs* also may be used to analyze characters. They differ from character maps in that the students record specific behaviors to support identified character traits. *Character perspective charts* prompt students to think about story elements from more than one point of view. Several *journal* formats are described in this chapter, all of which promote reactions and personal responses to reading selections. *Feelings charts* facilitate comprehension by providing a format for identifying and describing different viewpoints. *Contrast charts*, described in Chapter Two as a prereading activity, are appropriate for all phases of the instructional cycle, and they are included here so the reader may see examples of their application in another context and therefore gain a greater appreciation of their flexibility.

In summary, activities in this chapter are designed to:

- Facilitate students' comprehension
- Focus students' attention on particular themes, issues, or characters
- Encourage students to react to ideas, events, and characters
- Call students' attention to effective uses of language

■ Allow students to identify what they find most meaningful in a reading selection

Like the prereading activities described in Chapter Two, the activities discussed in this chapter require a response from each student and allow every student to experience success.

LITERATURE CIRCLES

Literature circles are temporary groupings of four or five students who meet regularly to discuss a piece of literature that all members of the group have chosen to read. Each group decides when and how long to meet and how much of the selection to read between meetings. Group members assign themselves specific responsibitilities for each upcoming discussion. These reponsibilities are rotated. When a group has completed the book, it decides whether and how to share it with the entire class. Then the group is disbanded.

Daniels (1994) provides several suggestions for group member responsibilities. Students may choose from among these, or the teacher may narrow the choices based upon the text and students' needs. One responsibility is to serve as Discussion Director. This student generates discussion questions based on the reading and leads the discussion when the group meets. The Literary Luminary (for works of fiction) and Passage Master (for nonfiction) locate three or four brief passages to real aloud and respond to with the group. Choices may include interesting ideas, humorous events, puzzling vocabulary, or important information; any reason for selecting a passage is acceptable. The Illustrator draws a picture or diagram that is related to the text. When sharing, the llustrator may first wish to ask group members what they believe the picture reveals. The Connector makes connections between the text and his or her own personal life, school life, events in the community, other writings, or anything that the Connector feels is appropriate. The Vocabulary Enricher selects vocabulary from the text that he or she wishes to share. Vocabulary choices may include unknown words, powerful words or phrases, or words that the author uses in an interesting way. The Travel Tracer's job is to record the movements of a character in the portion of text under discussion. This student writes a description or draws a map of a character's travels. The Investigator locates one or two pieces of information that are relevant to the reading. This may be information, for instance, about the author, the setting, or the time period.

Examples 3.1, 3.2, and 3.3 show the notes of a Discussion Director, Connector, and Passage Master for three different groups. These notes are not turned in to the group but, rather, are used to support the discussion.

Literature circles are useful for promoting students' responses to literature. By taking on a variety of roles in these groups, students develop appreciation for the multifaceted ways one might respond to a text. Students take ownership of their reading and the discussions and share what is meaningful to them. The literature circle experience allows students to make decisions about their reading, actively engage with the text and peers, explore ideas, and build and revise their understandings of the literature.

Example 3.1

- **Title:** *Mr. Popper's Penguins*
- **Author:** Richard and Florence Atwater
- **Grade Level:** 3–5
- **Summary:** Mr. Popper receives a penguin in the mail after sending a letter to an Arctic scientist. Mr. Popper and the penguin, named Captain Cook, have a number of hilarious adventures until the penguin's loneliness results in declining health. Soon Captain Cook is sent a mate, Greta, and nature takes its course, resulting in a house full of penguins. Mr. Popper takes the penguins on the road to perform their antics for audiences everywhere. Eventually, he makes the difficult decision to return the penguins to their natural habitat—and he accompanies them.

Discussion Director (Chapters 8–9)

What were these chapters about?

What would you think if you were getting your hair cut and someone came in with a penguin?

What do you think will happen now that Greta is there?

What would you do if you had a pet that became mopey?

Do you think Mr. Popper and Captain Cook will get into more trouble?

Example 3.2 _____

- **Title:** *Harry Potter and the Sorcerer's Stone*
- **Author:** J. K. Rowling
- **Grade Level:** 4–8
- **Summary:** Harry Potter has lived with the awful Dursley family for the first eleven years of his life and known only a miserable existence. Things change dramatically, however, when he receives a letter inviting him to attend the Hogwarts School of Witchcraft and Wizardry. There he makes friends, learns about magic, and finds himself involved in incredible adventures.

Connector (Chapter 1)

Self: *Mr. Dursley was afraid to mention the Potter's name to Mrs. Dursley because he knew she would get angry and upset. Sometimes, I am afraid to tell people certain things.*

Text: *I relate this book to the Magic Tree House series because there is magic. This book also reminds me of Roald Dahl's books because there are mean adults.*

World: *Like Mr. Dursley, there are people who don't like anyone who is different from them.*

Example 3.3 _____

- **Title:** *Talking with Artists, Vol. Three*
- **Author:** Pat Cummings
- **Grade Level:** 4–8
- **Summary:** The author asks a series of questions of 13 popular children's artists. Their answers are provided in this book.

Passage Master (pp. 28–39)

Quote: *p. 33—"Almost everyone in my books is based on someone I know. Friends, family, and even pets are often in my pictures. (No one who visits my house is safe.) . . . My husband was once given fairy wings and striped socks and has asked not to be used anymore."*

Why I picked this quote: *I picked this part because I think the artist has a good sense of humor. I laughed when I read her comment that no one who visits her house is safe. I could picture in my head her husband with fairy wings and striped socks, and I can just imagine him telling her no more pictures! I think it would be fun to be in one of her pictures—even if she dressed me in goofy clothes.*

LITERATURE MAPS

Literature maps, described by Haskell (1987), provide a means for responding to literature while reading. Literature maps are constructed by folding a piece of paper (8½-by-11-inch or larger) into four or more sections and labeling each section with a category name. Categories may include "setting," "themes," "predictions," "vocabulary," "questions," "symbols," "imagery," "reactions," or the names of characters. Categories are generally identified by the teacher. However, some students may like to create their own categories as they are reading.

The reader's task is to write category-related information in each section as he or she reads a chapter or a book. For example, given a section labeled "setting," the reader jots down words, phrases, or sentences about the setting of the story. It is not necessary for the student to record all data regarding a particular category. Rather, each student may include what he or she considers the most interesting or important information. A category such as "language" will yield diverse responses from students. Some students will write expressions they think are funny or unusual. Others may record words or phrases that confuse them. Still others may write descriptive phrases. As children bring their individuality to the literature, they will respond differently from one another.

Once the maps have been completed by individual students, they are shared. The teacher or group recorder draws a large map on a piece of butcher paper and asks the group members to contribute responses from their personal maps to the group map. Students may modify their personal maps while creating the group map.

As Haskell (1987) pointed out, the benefits of this activity are many. First, students become more actively involved in their reading. They paraphrase ideas and identify important or interesting information while they are reading. Second, discussion is enhanced. Because children have taken notes while reading, they are better prepared to discuss the traits or behaviors of a particular character, for example. Third, the students have a record to which they may refer when writing about the reading selection. Fourth, students have the opportunity to hear what their peers think is important or interesting. Fifth, students begin to notice language that is appealing or effective. They begin to comment, "I like the way the author described that"—a first step toward internalizing and modeling effective language. Sixth, a map may be constructed at several points in a book, and students can trace the development of the plot or of characters.

An additional and very important benefit of this activity is that all students can contribute to a group map and feel success as their ideas are included. For example, given a particular character, some students will simply respond with physical characteristics such as "has red hair" or "is 5 years old," while other students may generate higher-level responses such as "is considerate of others," "is a listener," or "appears to have a good self-concept." All responses should be recorded. Thus, all students will feel comfortable responding and should have something to contribute to the group map and follow-up discussion. When a higher-level response is given, the teacher should ask, "What makes you think so?" The student then must draw on incidents from the reading selection that led to his or her conclusions. By verbalizing his or her reasons, the student is modeling his or her thinking patterns for other students.

It is important that the teacher not overwhelm the students with too many categories. Further, the teacher must recognize that some students may find this activity disruptive to their reading, particularly if they feel the need to stop quite frequently to record information. We recommend that students who find this activity disruptive be allowed to listen to or read a selection in its entirety first, then complete the literature map during a second reading. Or, students may mark pages containing information related to literature map topics with self-adhesive paper. They return to these pages later to complete their literature maps.

Example 3.4 _____

- **Title:** *Ramona and Her Father*
- **Author:** Beverly Cleary
- **Grade Level:** 3–5
- **Summary:** Ramona's father loses his job, Ramona and Beezus go on a campaign to help him quit smoking, and Ramona practices acting so she can get a job on television commercials and earn enough money to help support her family.

Literature Map

Ramona	Her Father
happy	*lost his job*
making Christmas list	*worried*
loves gummy bears	*no fun anymore*
wants to help family	*patient*
practices commercials	*no money*
gets burs in hair	
Beezus	**Questions**
grouchy	*Will her father get another job?*
loves gummy bears	*Will her father be fun again?*
going through a phase	*Will Ramona be in commercials?*

Example 3.5 _____

- **Title:** *The History of Counting*
- **Author:** Denise Schmandt-Besserat
- **Grade Level:** 3–8
- **Summary:** The author provides fascinating information about the history of counting, including a variety of ways past cultures counted, the invention of the decimal counting system, and the advantages of this nearly universal system.

(continued)

Literature Map

Ways of Counting *counting without numbers* *body counting* *concrete counting* *abstract counting*	**Reasons for Counting Systems** *keep track of harvest and animals* *trade* *taxes*
Interesting Vocabulary *googol* *googolplex* *numerals* *bases* *decimal*	**Uses of Numbers in My Life** *sports* *telling time* *calendar* *cooking* *addresses* *buying things* *telephones*
Ways of Counting *notched bones* *tokens* *abstract symbols*	**Other Important Concepts** *place value*

Literature maps may be used at any grade level. A kindergarten teacher may modify the activity by leading a discussion and serving as recorder on a group map. The teacher may wish to read the book aloud in its entirety first. Then upon rereading, the teacher may ask students to listen for particular information in order to construct a literature map. Students may be asked to pay attention to the traits and actions of certain characters or to the setting, for instance. The teacher records students' ideas under these topics on the map. The teacher may ask students to identify what they are thinking or feeling at particular points in the story. These comments are included in a "Reactions" category.

Example 3.6 _____

- **Title:** *Are You My Mother?*
- **Author:** P. D. Eastman
- **Grade Level:** K–1

■ **Summary:** A little bird breaks out of his shell while his mother is away searching for food. The baby bird sets off to find his mother and asks a variety of animals and vehicles if they are his mother before he is reunited with her.

Literature Map

Mother Bird *cares about her baby* *goes off to find food*	**Baby Bird** *breaks out of shell* *leaves nest and falls* *can't fly* *wants to find his mother*
Possible Mothers *kitten steam shovel* *hen plane* *dog boat* *cow car*	**Questions** *Will the baby bird find his* *mother?* *Will the baby bird get hurt?* *Will the baby bird get lost?*

CHARACTER MAPS

Character maps may be used to help students recognize the traits of selected characters in a book as well as relationships between characters. After the students have read part of the book, the teacher or the students identify at least two characters for analysis. Each character's name is placed near the top of a circle or box on a single piece of paper. Students list character traits under each of the names. Thus, students may have several circles or boxes on a piece of paper, each with a name and list of traits underneath.

Next, the students draw an arrow from one character to another. Above and below the arrow, the students write words or phrases that tell how the first character feels about the second ("admires"), or what his or her relationship is to the second ("parent"). Several descriptors may be generated. A second arrow is drawn between these two characters, pointing in the opposite direction. Near this arrow the students write the second character's feelings about or relationship to the first.

Example 3.7 _____

- **Title:** *Charlotte's Web*
- **Author:** E. B. White
- **Grade Level:** 3–6
- **Summary:** Charlotte is a clever spider who befriends a pig named Wilbur and with the help of other animals saves him from a sure death.

Character Map (during Chapter Four)

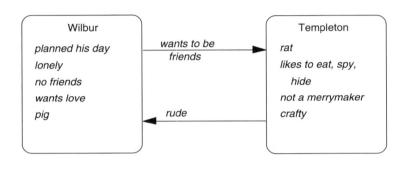

Character maps may be particularly useful in tracing the development of relationships. In the following example, two character maps are shown. The first was created by a class during the first part of the story. The second was written near the end of the story. These maps allow students to analyze the changes in characters as well as the changing relationships between characters.

Example 3.8 _____

- **Title:** *Mike Mulligan and His Steam Shovel*
- **Author:** Virginia L. Burton
- **Grade Level:** K–2
- **Summary:** Mike Mulligan is sad because he and his steam shovel, Mary Anne, have been replaced by new, modern equipment. In order to find work, he goes to a neighboring town where he meets Henry B. Swap who intends to trick

him into doing work for no pay. The story ends happily when Henry B. Swap appreciates Mike Mulligan's skills and stories.

Character Map (Story Beginning)

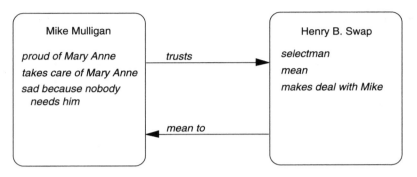

Character Map (Story Ending)

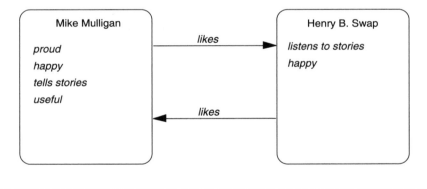

For more complex pieces of literature, several character maps might be developed. For example, in the book *Dragon's Gate*, by Laurence Yep, the young boy Otter greatly admires his Uncle Foxfire at the beginning of the book; is angry, bitter and disappointed with him later in the book; and then comes to understand and appreciate his uncle's courage and wisdom by the end of the book. The following three character maps illustrate changes that occur in the boy's perceptions of his uncle.

Example 3.9 _____

- **Title:** *Dragon's Gate*
- **Author:** Laurence Yep
- **Grade Level:** 5 and up
- **Summary:** Otter, a young Chinese boy, flees his country to join his legendary Uncle Foxfire and his father in America as they acquire new skills and knowledge by working on the transcontinental railroad. They plan to use this knowledge when they return to China to conduct the "Great Work." Otter is surprised by the working conditions and prejudice he encounters.

Character Map (Chapters 1–4)

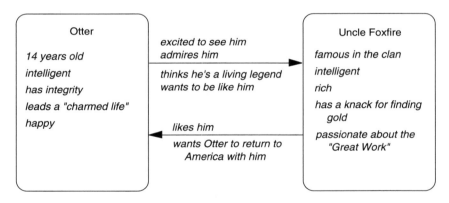

Character Map (Chapter 10)

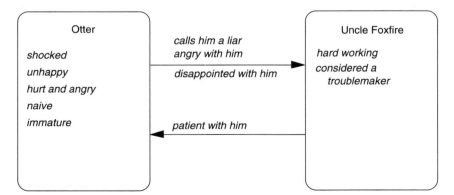

Character Map (Chapters 24–25)

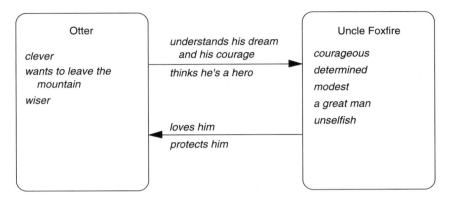

Otter		Uncle Foxfire
clever	*understands his dream and his courage*	courageous
wants to leave the mountain	*thinks he's a hero*	determined
wiser		modest
	loves him	a great man
	protects him	unselfish

CHARACTER WEBS

Another strategy for analyzing and prompting discussions about characters is the character web. In this strategy, students identify character traits and cite examples from the text as evidence. Bromley (1996) notes that webbing enhances comprehension and learning, links reading and writing, and promotes enjoyment. Character webs draw readers back to the text as they look for supporting examples, and so their interactions with the text are enriched.

Webs are very flexible instructional tools, and there are a great variety of web types. The examples included here have at the center the name of a character. Circles placed out from the center contain character traits. Shooting off from these circles are supporting facts or information drawn from the text. For example, in the book *Doctor DeSoto*, a character that might be analyzed is the doctor. Students might decide that he is clever, nice, cautious, and a good worker. After recording these traits in the circles, the students support their decisions by citing incidents from the story.

Example 3.10 _____

- **Title:** *Doctor DeSoto*
- **Author:** William Steig
- **Grade Level:** K–2

(continued)

- **Summary:** A mouse dentist and his wife typically refuse to take dangerous animals as patients. However, when they are approached by a suffering fox, they make an exception. They discover that they had better protect themselves from being eaten, and they devise a clever plan to outsmart the fox.

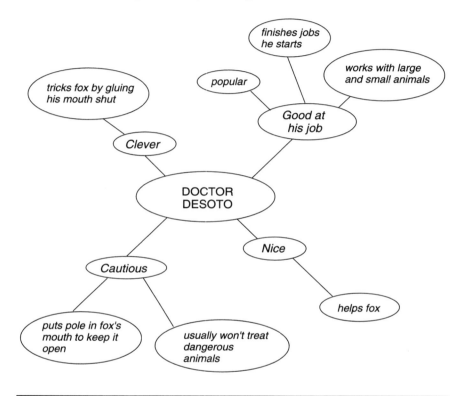

Example 3.11 _____

- **Title:** *Crazy Lady!*
- **Author:** Jane Leslie Conly
- **Grade Level:** 6 and up
- **Summary:** A boy whose life has changed after the death of his mother slowly befriends the local alcoholic and her retarded son.

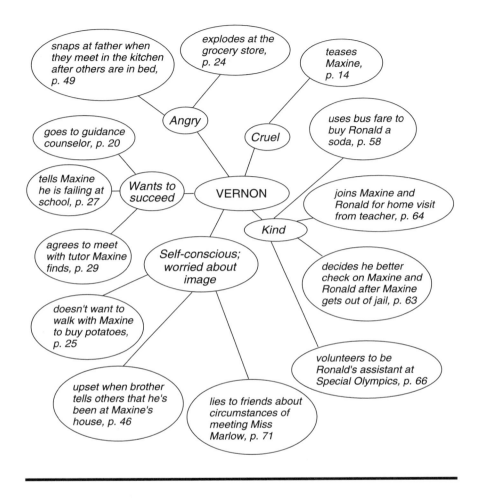

CHARACTER PERSPECTIVE CHARTS

Most narrative text follows what is known as story grammar, or a set of rules by which a story is structured. Stories have characters and occur in a particular setting. The main character has a goal or confronts a problem, engages in a number of activities to achieve the goal or overcome the problem, and ultimately, there is a resolution. Strategies that make story grammar explicit, such as story maps and charts in which students identify and record each of these elements of a narrative, help students create and remember stories and support comprehension development (Baumann &

Bergeron, 1993; Dickson, Simmons, & Kameenui, 1998; Dole, Brown, & Trathen, 1996; Leslie & Allan, 1999). However, it has been argued that story mapping can foster a misconception that there is only one possible interpretation of a story (Shanahan & Shanahan, 1997).

Character perspective charts (Shanahan & Shanahan, 1997) maintain the benefits of story mapping while at the same time promoting multiple interpretations. Instead of being focused on a single character and his or her problems, in character perspective charting, the students are guided to consider the story from more than one viewpoint.

Two examples of character perspective charts are displayed in Examples 3.12 and 3.13. In these examples, the teacher prepared a two-column chart that outlines the elements of story grammar in each column. In one column, the students responded to the prompts from one character's perspective, and in the other column, they responded to the prompts from a second character's perspective. Small groups of children who read the same book engaged in conversation and completed the chart together.

Example 3.12 _____

- **Title:** *Bread and Jam for Frances*
- **Author:** Russell Hoban
- **Grade Level:** 1–3
- **Summary:** Little Frances is interested in eating only her favorite food—bread and jam. She refuses to eat other foods that Mother prepares. She even trades away the lunch Mother packs for bread and jam sandwiches that her classmates have. Mother decides to let Francis eat only bread and jam for a while, and Frances discovers that eating only one type of food, even if it is a favorite, is not as desirable as it seems.

Character Perspective Chart

Main character: Who is the main character?	Main character: Who is the main character?
Frances	*Mother*

Setting: Where and when does the story take place?

at home and at school

Problem: What is the main character's problem?

her mother is serving foods other than her favorite bread and jam

Goal: What is the main character's goal? What does the character want?

she wants to eat only bread and jam

Attempt: What does the main character do to solve the problem or get the goal?

she trades her food for bread and jam

Outcome: What happens as a result of the attempt?

Frances becomes tired of eating only bread and jam and eagerly eats other foods

Reaction: How does the main character feel about the outcome?

happy

Theme: What point did the the author want to make?

try new things

Setting: Where and when does the story take place?

at home

Problem: What is the main character's problem?

her daughter won't try new foods

Goal: What is the main character's goal? What does the character want?

to get her daughter to try new new foods and eat a variety of foods

Attempt: What does the main character do to solve the problem or get the goal?

she serves other foods at first, then she only serves bread and jam to Frances

Outcome: What happens as a result of the attempt?

Frances tries other foods

Reaction: How does the main character feel about the outcome?

satisfied

Theme: What point did the the author want to make?

The best strategy may be to let people discover some things for themselves.

Example 3.13 _____

- **Title:** *Walk Two Moons*
- **Author:** Sharon Creech
- **Grade Level:** 5–8
- **Summary:** In this award-winning novel, thirteen-year-old Salamanca travels across the country with her grandparents to the site where her mother, having left home to find herself, was killed in a bus accident. Salamanca struggles with the fact that her mother left and will never return. While on the road trip, she tells her grandparents the story of her neighbor, Phoebe, whose mother also disappeared.

Character Perspective Chart

Main character: Who is the main character?	**Main character: Who is the main character?**
Salamanca Hiddle	*Phoebe Winterbottom*
Setting: Where and when does the story take place?	**Setting: Where and when does the story take place?**
on the road across the United States in the present	*in Euclid, Ohio in the present*
Problem: What is the main character's problem?	**Problem: What is the main character's problem?**
her mother left the family and is not returning	*there has been a strange boy looking for Mrs. Winterbottom; Mrs. Winterbottom is behaving oddly; Mrs. Winterbottom leaves the family*
Goal: What is the main character's goal? What does the character want?	**Goal: What is the main character's goal? What does the character want?**
she wants to reach her mother by her mother's birthday	*to have her mother come home; to find out who the boy is*
Attempt: What does the main character do to solve the problem or get the goal?	**Attempt: What does the main character do to solve the problem or get the goal?**

she goes on a car trip with her
grandparents, following her
mother's route

she tries to convince others that
the boy is a lunatic who has
kidnapped her mother; she goes
to the police; she tracks down
the boy

**Outcome: What happens as
a result of the attempt?**

she gets to Lewiston, her
mother's final destination, by
her mother's birthday

**Outcome: What happens as
a result of the attempt?**

no one believes her; her mother
soon returns with the boy and
everyone learns that the boy
is her son

**Reaction: How does the
main character feel about
the outcome?**

she accepts her mother's death
and understands that her
mother's decision to leave did
not mean that her mother did
not love her—the leaving was
something separate from her
love

**Reaction: How does the
main character feel about
the outcome?**

happy and angry

**Theme: What point did the
the author want to make?**

don't judge a man until you've
walked two moons in his
moccasins

**Theme: What point did the
the author want to make?**

don't judge a man until you've
walked two moons in his
moccasins

In a similar activity that combines story mapping with consideration of multiple perspectives, Emery (1996) recommends a three-
column chart. In the middle column, students record the story
problem, a list of important events that occur in the story, and the
resolution. A different character's name is put at the top of each of
the two remaining columns. Students engage in a discussion
about the characters' perspectives on each of the elements listed in
the middle column. Their ideas are recorded in the appropriate column immediately across from each of the story elements.

JOURNALS

Journals are a wonderful vehicle for integrating reading and writing. The act of writing in response to a reading selection helps to move both younger and older children beyond literal comprehension to a more complete understanding of the content of a book (Barone, 1989) and encourages personal, thoughtful engagement with books (Fuhler, 1994). There are many types of journals. Double-entry journals, reading logs, partner journals, and character journals will be described here.

The purpose of a double-entry journal is to allow students to select passages they find meaningful in a reading selection and then to write about why those passages are meaningful. Students may use $8\frac{1}{2}$-by-11-inch lined paper that has been folded in half lengthwise. In the left-hand column, the student summarizes interesting information or copies verbatim a sentence or paragraph of his of her own choosing from the reading selection and records the page number. Directly across from the text information or quote, in the right-hand column, the student reacts to the passage. Selections and responses will vary widely. Some passages may be selected because they are funny or use interesting language. Others may be selected because they touch the student's heart or remind the student of experiences in his or her own life.

This activity encourages interaction between the selection and the students and gives each student a chance to identify what is meaningful to him or her. Students may choose to share their responses with one another or to keep them private. The double-entry journal may be used effectively with children as young as first graders (Barone, 1990).

Example 3.14 _____

- **Title:** *Biggest, Strongest, Fastest*
- **Author:** Steve Jenkins
- **Grade Level:** K–3
- **Summary:** The author identifies animal record holders and provides some comparative information. The world's longest animal, for instance, is the sun jellyfish. Its poisonous tentacles, used to stun its prey, are over 200 feet long.

Double-Entry Journal

Interesting Information	Reponse
The strongest animal is an ant. It can carry five times its weight.	*I can't believe the ant is such a strong animal! I watch them in my yard. They do carry pretty big things.*

Example 3.15 _____

- **Title:** *Out of the Dust*
- **Author:** Karen Hesse
- **Grade Level:** 5–8
- **Summary:** Written as a free verse journal, this book provides a vivid description of life in the Oklahoma dust bowl during the Great Depression era. Fourteen-year-old Billie Jo struggles to help her family survive the conditions and the tragedy that takes her mother's life.

Double-Entry Journal

page 33

"The wind snatched that snow	*I can picture the dust*
right off the fields,	*coming across the land*
leaving behind a sea of dust,	*and covering everything.*
waves and	*I like the way Hesse placed*
waves and	*the words on the page. You can*
waves of	*almost feel the waves.*
dust,	*The image of dust coming out of your*
rippling across our yard.	*nose and mouth and eyes*
Daddy came in,	*really makes me understand*
he sat across from Ma and blew his nose.	*what it would be like to be in*
Mud streamed out.	*a dust storm. How frightening.*
He coughed and spit out	*How painful. Why would*
mud.	*anyone live there?*
If he had cried,	
his tears would have been mud too."	

Reading logs, or literature logs, are more structured than double-entry journals in that the teacher provides a prompt for writing following a period of sustained silent reading or a shared reading experience. Kelly and Farnan (1991) have argued that reading logs can be effective in promoting the critical thinking skills of analysis and evaluation and promoting personal interactions with text if the appropriate prompts are provided. Appropriate prompts are those that involve a reader's perception of, association with, or evaluation of the text. Kelly and Farnan provide a list of sixteen "reader-response" prompts, including the following: "What character was your favorite? Why?" "What character did you dislike? Why?" "Are you like any character in the story? Explain." "Does anything in this work remind you of your own life or something that happened to you?" "What was your first reaction to the story?" "If you were a teacher, would you read this book to your class?"

Each of these questions emphasizes the students' personal interpretations and interactions with the text. Non–reader-response prompts are those that focus exclusively on the text, such as "Tell me about your book." When the reader-response prompts were used with fourth-grade students, Kelly and Farnan found that students went beyond a literal response to the text and engaged in thinking that involved analysis of text from a variety of perspectives.

Example 3.16 _____

- **Title:** *Flip-Flop Girl*
- **Author:** Katherine Paterson
- **Grade Level:** 4–6
- **Summary:** When Vinnie's father dies, her brother stops speaking, and her mother can't make ends meet, the family moves across the county to live with Vinnie's grandmother. This book tells the story of the pain a young girl experiences when everything in her life seems to go wrong, and the special friendship that develops with a classmate who saves her brother.

Reading Log

Prompt (after reading Chapter Two):

Does anything in this chapter remind you of something that has happened to you?

Response:

I guess I'm really lucky. I have been going to this school since kindergarten. I can just imagine how awful it would be to leave your friends and move to a new place. I wouldn't want to be brand-new in a school where everybody else already knows each other. Vinnie must feel terrible, especially with everything else that's going on in her life. And that Heather girl was mean. I'm glad that the teacher seems so nice.

Partner journals (sometimes referred to as dialogue journals) require students to interact with another person, often a peer. The students may react to a chapter after it is read or the teacher may offer prompts. Once the writing is completed, students exchange journals with a partner who responds to their comments. This exchange may occur immediately or after a day or two have elapsed. Partners may be anonymous, each student having a secret identification number or name, or may be known. If two classes are reading the same book, journals may be exchanged across classes. Partner journals stimulate purposeful communication, provide an opportunity for writing, and allow for feedback from peers (Bromley, 1989). Morgan and Albritton (1990) reported success with this activity with children as young as second graders and found that both the content and the form of student writing improved over time.

Example 3.17 _____

- **Title:** *A Gathering of Days*
- **Author:** Joan Blos
- **Grade Level:** 4–6
- **Summary:** Written in journal format, this book tells the story of two years in the life of a nineteenth-century New England girl.

Partner Journal

Dear Journal Partner:

This book is so cool! I have a diary, but I'm not very good about writing in it. Do you suppose someone will want to publish it someday?! Who do you think "the phantom" is that she has seen twice now?

Your Partner

Dear Partner:

I don't know who the phantom is. The book tells about bound boys who should be returned when they run away. Do you suppose the phantom is a boy who ran away? I wonder if Aunt Lucy is going to end up marrying the father.

I don't have a diary, but I think it would be fun to write in one. You could tell secrets to your diary that you wouldn't dare tell anyone else!

Your Partner

Parents can be included in the journal experience also. If the parent has read the same book, the two can respond to the literature sharing their points of view and their reactions. If the parent has not read the book, then he or she may respond to the child's comments by asking questions, requesting clarification, and reacting to the child's comments. In example 3.18, a second-grade child read *Sea Turtles* in class, wrote in his partner journal, then took the book and the journal home to his parents. Both parents chose to respond. The book and journal were returned to school several days later. The boy waited until he was at school to read his parents' responses.

Fuhler (1994) describes an experience she had with her junior high students and their parents in which the parents were invited to read the same book as their children and to participate in a dialogue about the book through the use of a partner journal. She found that most parents were delighted to be involved in the activity, and she was impressed with the thoughtful responses made by both parents and students.

Example 3.18 _____

- **Title:** *Sea Turtles*
- **Author:** Gail Gibbons
- **Grade Level:** K–2
- **Summary:** The author describes the variety of sea turtles, discusses their habits, explains people's efforts to protect them, and compares them to land turtles. This book is rich in information and a useful resource for young readers.

Partner Journal

Dear Mom and Dad:

I like reading about sea turtles. They are my favorite animal. Did you know they live a long, long time? Can I see one sometime?

Dear Son:

This was an interesting book! It is fascinating that sea turtles can live to be over 100 years old! I learned other things about sea turtles that I never knew. For instance, I didn't know that sea turtles have been around for millions of years. Wow! I also didn't know that they lay about 100 eggs at a time! Imagine a human mother having 100 babies!!

I hope we will see a sea turtle sometime. Maybe we can go to the aquarium soon.

Love,

Dad

(continued)

Dear Son,

I had desert tortoises when I was young. They used to hibernate in the winter. We never knew quite where they went— one day we'd go outside and couldn't find them. Then, months later, they'd reappear! I learned from your book that sea turtles disappear too! They don't hibernate, but they do migrate—travel a long distance away—when they are going to have their young.
Share another book with me soon!

Love,

Mom

In character journals, suggested by Hancock (1993) and Van Horn (1997), the students assume the voice of a character in a book as they record their feelings about story events. Hancock argues that when students are encouraged "to step inside [a character's] mind and heart and compose a personal response from his [or her] point of view" (p. 42), a high level of involvement and identification is attained. Readers grow in their understanding of the actions, motives, and emotions of the character. Hancock found in working with her eighth-grade students that they also needed the opportunity to react from their own perspectives, however. Students' personal entries can be set off in parentheses to distinguish them from the voice of the main character. By thinking about story events from both the character's perspective and their own perspectives, students may gain insights into their own values and ideals, thus gaining a greater sense of their identities—adding a powerful dimension to this type of journal.

Example 3.19 _____

- **Title:** *Shiloh*

- **Author:** Phyllis Reynolds Naylor

- **Grade Level:** 4–6

- **Summary:** A young boy growing up in West Virginia discovers that a neighbor is abusing a dog. In his efforts to save the dog, the boy struggles with a number of moral dilemmas.

Character Journal

Student entry (during Chapter Two):

I can't stand it. Dad's making me take this dog back to that mean Judd Travers. Poor dog. I can tell he ain't been treated right. I can't believe Dad says it's no mind of ours how Judd treats the dog. The dog is shaking, he's so scared. How can Dad do this? What if the dog were a kid? What would Dad do then? What can I do to convince him not to take the dog back?

(How awful. I don't understand how people can be mean to animals, or how other people can let them get by with it. I know my mom would let me help a mistreated animal! She loves animals.)

It is important that teachers emphasize communication when using journals or logs in the classroom. Teachers should limit correction of students' spelling, punctuation, and syntax and model standard usage as they respond in writing to the content of students' entries. Students will begin to modify their own spellings to match the conventions used by the teacher (Bode, 1989). Yet because the focus is on the message, not the form, students will be freed to think about ideas. Responses should be nonjudgmental, encouraging, and thought stretching (Fuhler, 1994; Hancock, 1993).

Journals provide readers with the opportunity to think about and share their feelings and thoughts about characters, events, and ideas throughout their reading of a book. They give students a voice in their reading, and allow them to collaborate with an author as they create meaning together (Fuhler, 1994). A variety of journal formats should be used throughout the course of a school year, because each type provides a different kind of experience for both the teacher and the student. Double-entry journals, reading logs, partner journals, and character journals are just four journal formats. Edwards (1991–92) describes several other exciting formats that she claims are useful in promoting critical thinking skills.

FEELINGS CHARTS

A feelings chart is useful in helping students analyze characters' reactions to one or more events in a piece of literature. The chart also may serve as a vehicle for comparing and contrasting characters and is beneficial in building vocabulary.

The teacher prepares by identifying several events that occur in the reading selection and then listing the characters who are influenced by the event. Events are listed, as in Example 3.20, down the side of a chart. Characters are listed across the top of the chart. As the students read or listen to a selection, they are asked to provide a one-word description of each character's feelings at the time of each event. Their descriptions are written where the respective characters and the events intersect on the chart.

Example 3.20 _____

- **Title:** *The Wave*
- **Author:** Margaret Hodges
- **Grade Level:** 2–3
- **Summary:** The people of a village in Japan are threatened by a destructive tidal wave. Only an old man who resides at the top of a hill sees the danger. He attempts to warn the villagers by burning his precious rice fields.

Feelings Chart

Events	Characters		
	Ojiisan	Tada	Villagers
The water was calm and the village children played in the gentle waves.	*content* *satisfied* *happy*	*glad* *happy* *playful*	*thankful* *secure* *lucky* *peaceful* *cheerful*
Ojiisan sets fire to the rice fields.	*awful* *bad* *sad* *worried*	*anxious* *puzzled* *curious* *upset* *horrified*	*excited* *surprised* *unlucky* *vengeful* *angry* *crazy*
The huge tidal wave strikes the beach.	*afraid* *hopeful* *thankful*	*scared* *afraid* *panic*	*scared* *frightened* *terrified* *afraid*

The villagers, Ojisan, and Tada look down upon the empty beach where their village used to stand.	*successful* *relieved* *right*	*proud* *amazed*	*lucky* *thankful* sad *dazed* *forgiving* *grateful* *horrified* *amazed* *shocked*

This activity may be conducted using a large chart in the front of the classroom with the teacher directing the entire activity and the students participating in a whole-class discussion. Alternative patterns include the use of small groups, pairs of students, or even individuals who complete their own charts and then later share their responses with the entire class.

Three student teachers modeled an interesting approach to this activity in a university seminar. The student teachers displayed the chart identifying key events in the story in the front of the room and then read the book aloud, pausing after each event. At each pause, they distributed small sheets of paper to everyone in the class and directed those students sitting on the right side of the classroom to write a single word that described how Ojiisan felt at the time. Students in the center of the classroom each wrote a word describing how Tada felt, and those students on the left side of the classroom wrote a word describing the feelings of the villagers. Each member of the class was permitted to write only one word. Then students, one row at a time, were instructed to bring their paper to the chart and stick it on the chart in the appropriate place. (Self-sticking paper was used, which saved an enormous amount of time.) After all papers had been displayed, each contribution was read and discussed. The variety of words generated by the class was astounding, and the reaction from the students was one of interest and curiosity. The responses in Example 3.20 are a sampling of those given by the university students.

Some students may wish to include a column labeled "Me" so they have an opportunity to respond to the events as well.

Example 3.21 _____

- **Poem:** "Casey at the Bat"
- **Book:** *The Family Book of Best Loved Poems* (David L. George, ed.)
- **Poet:** Ernest Lawrence Thayer
- **Grade Level:** 5 and up
- **Summary:** Fans count on Casey to win the baseball game. When he strikes out, it is a sad day in the history of Mudville.

Feelings Chart

Events	Characters		
	Casey	The Crowd	Me
Casey steps up to bat.			
The umpire calls, "Strike Two!"			
Casey strikes out.			

CONTRAST CHARTS

Contrast charts were described in Chapter Two as a prereading activity. These charts also may be used during reading as a means for recording contrasting ideas or information in a selection as it is read. For example, students may list the pros and cons of an issue, the advantages and disadvantages of a course of action, or the two sides of an argument as they are described in the selection. Once information from the selection has been organized in this manner, the chart may serve as a guide for writing. In Example 3.22, children record a character's reasons for and against taking a teddy bear to a sleepover while they are reading or listening to the story.

Example 3.22 _____

- **Title:** *Ira Sleeps Over*
- **Author:** Bernard Waber
- **Grade Level:** K–3
- **Summary:** Ira has been invited to spend the night at a friend's house. He is very excited until his sister asks him whether he plans to take along his teddy bear. Ira wrestles with this question because he doesn't want to appear babyish to his friend, but he has never slept without "TaTa."

Contrast Chart

Reasons Why Ira Should Take His Teddy Bear	Reasons Why Ira Should Not Take His Teddy Bear
He's never slept without it.	*His friend will laugh at him.*
They're going to tell scary stories.	*He'll think Ira is a baby.*
His friend's house is very dark.	*His friend will laugh at the bear's name.*

Example 3.23 _____

- **Title:** *Call of the Wild*
- **Author:** Jack London
- **Grade Level:** 7 and above

(continued)

■ **Summary:** Buck is a well-cared-for family dog who is removed from his comfortable home in the south to serve as sled dog in the Alaskan wilderness.

Contrast Chart

Life in the South	Life in the North
1.	1.
2.	2.
3.	3.
4.	4.
5.	5.

CONCLUSION

Literature circles, literature maps, character maps, character webs, character perspective charts, journals, feelings charts, and contrast charts may be used during reading as means to facilitate comprehension and to focus attention on content or language. Perhaps even more important, several of these activities provide students with the opportunity to react to a literature selection from a personal point of view and to identify what they find most meaningful.

REFERENCES

Atwater, R., & Atwater, F. (1966). *Mr. Popper's penguins*. New York: Little, Brown.

Barone, D. (1989). Young children's written responses to literature: The relationship between written response and orthographic knowledge. In S. McCormick & J. Zutell (Eds.), *Cognitive and social perspectives for literacy research and instruction* (pp. 371–379). Chicago: National Reading Conference.

Barone, D. (1990). The written responses of young children: Beyond comprehension to story understanding. *The New Advocate, 3*(1), 49–56.

Baumann, J. F., & Bergeron, B. S. (1993). Story map instruction using children's literature: Effects on first graders' comprehension of central narrative elements. *Journal of Reading Behavior, 25*, 407–437.

Blos, J. W. (1979). *A gathering of days*. New York: Macmillan.

Bode, B. (1989). Dialogue journal writing. *The Reading Teacher, 42,* 568–571.

Bromley, K. (1989). Buddy journals make the reading-writing connection. *The Reading Teacher, 43,* 122–129.

Bromley, K. (1996). *Webbing with literature: Creating story maps with children's books.* Boston: Allyn and Bacon.

Burton, V. L. (1967). *Mike Mulligan and his steam shovel.* Boston: Houghton Mifflin.

Cleary, B. (1975). *Ramona and her father.* New York: Dell.

Conly, J. L. (1993). *Crazy lady!* New York: HarperCollins.

Creech, S. (1996). *Walk two moons.* New York: HarperTrophy.

Cummings, P. (1999). *Talking with artists, Vol. 3.* New York: Clarion.

Daniels, H. (1994). *Literature circles: Voice and choice in the student-centered classroom.* York, ME: Stenhouse.

Dickson, S. V., Simmons, D. C., & Kameenui, E. J. (1998). Text organization: Research bases. In D. C. Simmons & E. J. Kameenui (Eds.), *What reading research tells us about children with diverse learning needs: Bases and basics.* (pp. 239–277). Mahwah, NJ: Lawrence Erlbaum.

Dole, J. A., Brown, K. J., & Trathen, W. (1996). The effects of strategy instruction on the comprehension performance of at-risk students. *Reading Research Quarterly, 31,* 62–88.

Eastman, P. D. (1960). *Are you my mother?* New York: Beginner Books.

Edwards, P. (1991–92). Using dialectical journals to teach thinking skills. *Journal of Reading, 35,* 312–316.

Emery, D. (1996). Helping readers comprehend stories from the characters' perspectives. *The Reading Teacher, 49*(7), 9 534-541.

Fuhler, C. (1994). Response journals: Just one more time with feeling. *Journal of Reading, 37,* 400–405.

Gibbons, G. (1995). *Sea turtles.* New York: Holiday House.

Hancock, M. (1993). Character journals: Initiating involvement and identification through literature. *Journal of Reading, 37,* 42–50.

Haskell, S. (1987). Literature mapping. *The California Reader, 20,* 29–31.

Hesse, K. (1997). *Out of the dust.* New York: Scholastic.

Hoban, R. (1993). *Bread and jam for Frances.* New York: HarperCollins.

Hodges, M. (1964). *The wave.* Boston: Houghton Mifflin.

Jenkins, S. (1995). *Biggest, strongest, fastest.* New York: Scholastic.

Kelly, P., & Farnan, N. (1991). Promoting critical thinking through response logs: A reader-response approach with fourth graders. In J. Zutell & S. McCormick (Eds.), *Learner Factors/Teacher Factors: Issues in Literacy Research and Instruction.* Fortieth Yearbook of the National Reading Conference. Chicago: The National Reading Conference.

Leslie, L., & Allen, L. (1999). Factors that predict success in an early literacy intervention project. *Reading Research Quarterly, 34,* 404–424.

London, J. (1974). *Call of the wild.* New York: Simon & Schuster.

Morgan, R., & Albritton, J. D. (1990). Primary students respond to literature through partner journals. *The California Reader, 23,* 29–30.

Naylor, P. R. (1991). *Shiloh.* New York: Atheneum.

Parker, S. (1999). *It's an ant's life.* Pleasantville, NY: Reader's Digest Children's Books.

Paterson, K. (1994). *Flip-flop girl.* New York: Lodestar.

Pearson, P. D., & Fielding, L. (1991). Comprehension instruction. In R. Barr, M. L. Kamil, P. Mosenthal, & P. D. Pearson (Eds.), *Handbook of reading research* (Vol. 2, pp. 815–860). White Plains, NY: Longman.

Rosenblatt, L. (1978). *The reader, the text, the poem: The transactional theory of the literary word.* Carbondale: Southern Illinois University Press.

Rowling, J. K. (1997). *Harry Potter and the sorcerer's stone.* New York: Arthur A. Levine.

Schmandt-Besserat, D. (1999). *The history of counting.* New York: Morrow Junior Books.

Shanahan, T., & Shanahan, S. (1997). Character Perspective Charting: Helping children to develop a more complete conception of story. *The Reading Teacher, 50,* 668–677.

Steig, W. (1982). *Doctor DeSoto.* New York: Farrar, Straus & Giroux.

Thayer, E. L. (1952). Casey at the bat. In David L. George (Ed.), *The family book of best loved poems* (pp. 411–412). Garden City, NY: Hanover House.

Van Horn, L. (1997). The characters within us: Readers connect with characters to create meaning and understanding. *Journal of Adolescent and Adult Literacy, 40,* 342–347.

Waber, B. (1975). *Ira sleeps over.* Boston: Houghton Mifflin.

White, E. B. (1952). *Charlotte's web.* New York: Harper & Row.

Yep, L. (1993). *Dragon's gate.* New York: HarperCollins.

CHAPTER FOUR

Postreading Activities

Postreading

Purposes

- To encourage reflection
- To facilitate analysis and synthesis
- To promote personal responses and connections to ideas, themes, and issues encountered in the book
- To extend comprehension
- To facilitate organization of information

Activities

- Polar opposites
- Quotation shares
- Literary report cards
- Plot organizers
- World wheels
- Venn diagrams
- Book charts

The postreading activities students engage in will have an impact on how they view the reading selection as well as the reading act. If students reflect on important ideas, share reactions, return to the book to achieve greater understanding, make connections between what they have just learned and what they already knew, and use what was learned in a personally meaningful way, the selection will be viewed as a source of enjoyment and will be long remembered. Reading will be viewed as a meaning-based activity. If, on the other hand, students respond to a series of low-level questions, work quietly, prove that they can sequence events by numbering them on a worksheet, and complete a crossword puzzle to reinforce vocabulary, then they are likely to view the selection as simply a vehicle for skills instruction. Reading will be perceived as a skills-based activity.

The postreading activities we provide in this chapter are intended to be in keeping with the reasons for using literature in the classroom. In particular, they promote enjoyment of reading and stimulate thoughtful interaction with text. All of the activities encourage reflection on some aspect of the text, such as characters, important ideas or events, themes, issues, or concepts. Many facilitate analysis and synthesis of ideas. Some provide a vehicle for integration of prior knowledge and new information and promote the extension of students' comprehension beyond the book itself by helping students make connections across books, authors, and with their own lives. The activities facilitate the organization of ideas and provide a structure for meaningful discussion in which all students may share their ideas and interpretations.

The first activity, *polar opposites*, gives students a framework for thinking about characters or concepts. It requires analysis of characters' behaviors and the author's language in order to draw conclusions about traits. *Quotation shares* prompt students to think about interesting or powerful ideas, events, and language in a book. *Literary report cards* provide a motivating format for thinking about and discussing characters. *Plot organizers* provide a graphic means for organizing and analyzing the plot of a story. *World wheels* are a vehicle for summarizing and organizing information from books with multicultural themes. *Venn diagrams* facilitate comparisons between two or more characters, events, or books, or between a character and the readers themselves. *Book charts* are useful for examining several books by the same author or with the same theme.

Thus, the postreading activities presented in this chapter may be used to:

- Encourage reflection on ideas, themes, and issues encountered in the book
- Facilitate analysis and synthesis of ideas
- Promote personal responses and connections to ideas, themes, and issues encountered in the book
- Extend comprehension beyond the immediate text
- Facilitate organization of information

POLAR OPPOSITES

This activity may be used to help students analyze characters in a reading selection by asking them to rate one or more characters on a variety of dimensions along three-, five-, or seven-point scales. It is most effective when students are asked to draw examples from the text to support their responses. In other words, students may not simply rate a character as "passive" rather than "aggressive." They must also provide reasons for their ratings.

To develop a polar opposites guide, the teacher should begin by selecting a character and developing a list of qualities or characteristics that describe him or her. Then the teacher thinks of the opposite of each of those qualities. For example, if a character is very sure of himself, has many friends, and is easily angered, the list might include "confident," "popular," and "hot-tempered." Opposites of these might be "unsure," "unpopular," and "easygoing." (Opposites used will depend on the precise meaning intended by the initial term.) Each pair of opposites makes up its own continuum, as seen in the examples that follow. After reading a selection, students are asked to rate the character(s) by placing a mark on each continuum. In Example 4.1, we have placed an X on each continuum to show possible student responses. Please keep in mind that responses will vary.

Example 4.1 _____

- **Poem:** "The Road Not Taken"
- **Book:** *You Come Too* (Robert Frost)
- **Poet:** Robert Frost
- **Grade Level:** 4 and up
- **Summary:** A traveler reflects on his decision to take a less traveled road.

Polar Opposites

The traveler was

thoughtful	_X_	____	____	____	impulsive
timid	____	____	____	_X_	courageous
disappointed	____	____	____	_X_	content
realistic	____	_X_	____	____	unrealistic
a follower	____	____	____	_X_	a leader

Nowhere in the poem does the poet explicitly state that the traveler is thoughtful or impulsive, timid or courageous, disappointed or content, and so on. Students must examine the traveler's behaviors and thoughts in order to form a judgment. We have used this particular polar opposites activity with many groups and find it leads to considerable discussion and analysis of the poet's language.

Students support their responses in discussions. Additionally, they may write or dictate to the teacher the reasons for each rating, as in Example 4.2. It is important to remember that any rating is acceptable as long as the student is able to support his or her response with information from the text.

Note that in Example 4.2 a three-point scale rather than a five-point scale is used. *The Story of Ferdinand* is likely to be used with kindergarten children who may have difficulty with a five-point scale. The teacher must decide how many points to include on a polar opposites scale based on his or her knowledge of the students.

Example 4.2 _____

- **Title:** *The Story of Ferdinand*
- **Author:** Munro Leaf
- **Grade Level:** K–1
- **Summary:** Ferdinand the bull is very different from other bulls. He is big and strong, but he is not interested in butting heads and fighting. He prefers to sit and smell flowers.

Polar Opposites

Ferdinand is

happy ___X___ _____ _____ sad

He seems to be very happy as long as he can sit and smell flowers. He was even happy in the bull's ring because he could smell the flowers in the ladies' hair.

healthy ___X___ _____ _____ unhealthy

He is big and strong which means he must be healthy.

fierce _____ _____ ___X___ tame

Ferdinand likes to sit. He is not interested in fighting.

same _____ _____ ___X___ different

Ferdinand is different from other bulls. He is happy sitting while the others like to fight and butt heads. He was not interested in being picked for the bull's ring. Other bulls did try hard to be picked.

brave ___X___ _____ _____ fearful

(continued)

He must be fairly brave because he did what he wanted to do even though it was not like other bulls. Also, he did not seem upset about going into the bull's ring.

A modification of a polar opposites guide is presented in Example 4.3. In *From the Mixed-Up Files of Mrs. Basil E. Frankweiler*, two characters have contrasting traits and may be rated along the same dimensions. Students are to write a "C" for Claudia and a "J" for Jamie at the appropriate point on each continuum.

Example 4.3 _____

- **Title:** *From the Mixed-Up Files of Mrs. Basil E. Frankweiler*
- **Author:** E. L. Konigsburg
- **Grade Level:** 5–6
- **Summary:** Two children, Claudia and Jamie, run away from home and hide in a museum where they solve a mystery.

Polar Opposites

tightwad	_J_	____	____	_C_	big spender
cautious	____	_C_	_J_	____	adventurous
predictable	____	_C_	____	_J_	spontaneous
messy	_J_	____	____	_C_	neat and tidy
organized	_C_	____	____	_J_	disorganized

Polar opposites may be used successfully with all age groups to facilitate readers' reflection on characters in a piece of literature. They offer a structure for discussions and can serve as a prewriting activity. They encourage critical thinking, as students must analyze and synthesize what they know about a character in order to make judgments.

Example 4.4 _____

- **Title:** *The Watsons Go to Birmingham—1963*
- **Author:** Christopher Paul Curtis
- **Grade Level:** 5–8
- **Summary:** In this humorous and deeply moving book, we come to know the Watsons—a black family living in Michigan—from the point of view of ten-year-old Kenny. Kenny has a little sister, Joetta, and an older brother, Byron, whom he considers a juvenile delinquent. Byron's behavior concerns his parents and they decide to take him to Alabama to spend the summer with his grandmother, hoping that by removing him from his friends and placing him with this strong woman, he will change. The year is 1963, the height of the civil rights movement and a time of tension and confrontation, and together the Watsons take the long road trip to the South. The family, particularly Kenny, is devastated when a church in Alabama where Joetta is attending Sunday school is bombed. Byron plays an important role in helping Kenny recover. This book is a multiple-award winner.

Polar Opposites

Byron is

mean	___	___	___	___	___	kind
insensitive	___	___	___	___	___	sensitive
disrespectful	___	___	___	___	___	respectful
not likable	___	___	___	___	___	likable
unintelligent	___	___	___	___	___	intelligent

QUOTATION SHARES

The quotation share activity (similar to "read arounds" described by Tompkins, 1997) provides students who have read the same book with an opportunity to share excerpts they find compelling or interesting. Each student revisits the literature, skimming the work for a selection he or she wishes to share. After some time to rehearse their selections, students come together and read aloud their selections one at a time. One student voluntarily reads his or her passage, then another student reads. Students are not called upon, nor is a particular order followed. Students read their selection whenever they are so moved, and no one is forced to share. As the reading moves from one passage to another, no time is taken for discussion. The students are silent as they listen to each passage. Teachers find that students become engrossed as the group weaves back and forth through the literature, reexperiencing portions of the book together. There are, of course, no "correct," "incorrect," "good," or "poor" choices. Quotation choices are personal.

After the sharing, students discuss the experience and comment on the selections. Students gain insights into the thinking of their peers and appreciation for the author's writing as peers explain why they found certain passages compelling or interesting. They notice commonalities and differences in their choices and thinking. They notice the author's techniques for capturing the reader.

An alternative to the oral sharing of personally selected quotations is a written sharing. Participants select a passage to share and copy it onto a piece of paper. These papers are then displayed around the classroom; the room becomes a gallery of quotations. At a given time, the teacher and students silently meander around the room to read the passages, carrying pencils so that they may write a response on any of the papers. Responses may be brief or lengthy and often take the form of comments such as "Oh, yes! I really enjoyed this part, too!" "I felt so bad when I read this part," "This was very funny! I like how the author spelled the words in the section to exaggerate the sounds," "Many of us selected this same passage!" "This really makes you think about how lucky you are and how much we don't know about other people in the world." "I was stunned when I read this section. It came so suddenly and was so unexpected. The book seemed so lighthearted at first, then changed with a few words." After the gallery walk, the group discusses the experience as they did for the oral sharing.

LITERARY REPORT CARDS

Literary report cards provide children with an entertaining vehicle for analysis of characters. In this activity, suggested by Johnson and Louis (1987), students are given the opportunity to issue grades to characters in a reading selection. Initially, the teacher may select the "subjects" on which the characters will be graded. Rather than academic areas, characters may be graded on personality traits, such as "courageous" or "patient." (Eventually, the students may generate the subject areas. Selection of subject areas requires higher-level thinking, as the students must reflect on the character, analyze his or her qualities and behavior, and label the qualities.) In addition to awarding the grades, students comment on or cite evidence for each grade. Report cards themselves may be modeled after real report cards used at the school that the students attend.

Example 4.5

- **Title:** *The Indian in the Cupboard*
- **Author:** Lynn Reid Banks
- **Grade Level:** 5–8
- **Summary:** When Omri puts a plastic Indian toy into a cupboard, it becomes a real live person. This book tells the story of Omri's adventures with the Indian and relates what an enormous responsibility it is to take care of another person.

Literary Report Card

S.M. All Elementary School

Student: Omri

Area	Grade	Comment
arts and crafts	A	*Omri constructed a beautiful tepee for the Indian.*
respect for others	A	*Omri valued the Indian as a real person with real feelings.*
creativity	A	*Omri solved many problems, such as how to feed and provide shelter for the Indian.*
responsibility	A	*Omri took excellent care of Little Bear.*
attentiveness in school	C	*Omri spent too much time thinking about Little Bear.*

For primary-grade children, descriptors such as "good," "satisfactory," and "needs to improve" may be more appropriate than letter grades.

Example 4.6 _____

- **Title:** *Nate the Great*
- **Author:** Marjorie Weinman Sharmat
- **Grade Level:** K–2
- **Summary:** Nate the Great is a detective whose job is to find a missing picture.

Literary Report Card

Gumshoe Elementary School		
Student: Nate		
G—Good S—Satisfactory N—Needs to Improve		
Area	Grade	Comments
believes in himself	G	*is sure that he can find Annie's lost picture*
can be counted on	G	*leaves a note for his mother when he leaves the house, takes his job very seriously*
is smart	G	*makes plan for finding picture, figures that the only place Fang could bury something is in the backyard, knows red and yellow make orange, figures out where the picture is*
is patient	S	*digs for two hours in the backyard but is in a hurry to leave Rosamond's house and gets mad when Harry paints him*

Example 4.7 _____

- **Title:** *The Tale of Peter Rabbit*
- **Author:** Beatrix Potter
- **Grade Level:** K–2
- **Summary:** Peter Rabbit disobeys his mother and goes to Mr. McGregor's garden. There he is chased by Mr. McGregor and barely escapes.

Literary Report Card

O'Hare Private School		
Student: Peter		
G—Good S—Satisfactory	N—Needs to Improve	
Areas	Grade	Comments
obedience	N	*He went to Mr. McGregor's garden even though his mother told him not to.*
bravery	N	*He cried a lot when he got caught in a net and when he couldn't find his way out of the garden.*
sports	G	*He ran fast, jumped into a bucket and out of a window, and wiggled under a fence.*

Any grade should be accepted as long as the child is able to provide a reason for the grade. In Example 4.7, some students may give Peter Rabbit an "S" or a "G" in bravery rather than an "N," stating that he was brave to go into McGregor's garden. It is important that the teacher not have correct answers in mind. Rather, he or she must look for reasonable, thoughtful responses and examine students' abilities to substantiate their claims.

It is important that all graded areas be stated in the positive form. It makes no sense to award a character an "A" in impatience, for example, or a "D" in dishonesty.

PLOT ORGANIZERS

Plot organizers provide a visual display of the events that occur in a story. They are useful for helping students summarize a plot and understand its organization, and they also can serve as a model for students' original work (see Chapter Five).

Two plot patterns that may be found in young children's books are the circular and the cumulative patterns. These can be depicted as shown in Examples 4.8 and 4.9.

Example 4.8 _____

- **Title:** *If You Give a Mouse a Cookie*
- **Author:** Laura Joffe Numeroff
- **Grade Level:** K–2
- **Summary:** A young boy describes the cycle of events that could take place if you give a mouse a cookie.

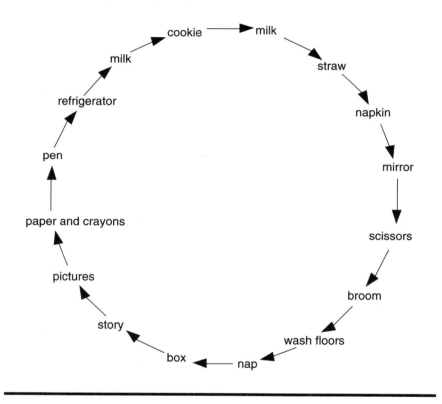

Example 4.9 _____

- **Title:** *This Is the House Where Jack Lives*
- **Author:** Joan Heilbroner
- **Grade Level:** K–2
- **Summary:** This cumulative story tells the consequences of the flooding caused by the overflowing bathtub in which Jack plays.

											Jack
										water	water
									lady	lady	lady
								cook	cook	cook	cook
							cat	cat	cat	cat	cat
						girl	girl	girl	girl	girl	girl
					mop	mop	mop	mop	mop	mop	mop
				man	man	man	man	man	man	man	man
			pail	pail	pail	pail	pail	pail	pail	pail	pail
		boy	boy	boy	boy	boy	boy	boy	boy	boy	boy
	dog	dog	dog	dog	dog	dog	dog	dog	dog	dog	dog
house	house	house	house	house	house	house	house	house	house	house	house

Some cumulative stories, such as *The Napping House*, by Audrey Wood, build to a point and then recede, first adding elements one at a time and then eliminating those elements one at a time until the story ends. This kind of plot structure could be displayed in a stair-step pattern that first rises and then falls. Stair-step organizers also may be used for countdown books such as *Five Little Ducks*, by Ian Beck, and *Five Little Monkeys Jumping on the Bed*, by Eileen Christelow. The stairs are positioned in descending order from left to right.

A plot profile (Johnson & Louis, 1987; see also DeGroff & Galda, 1992) is a more complex type of plot organizer. Students identify the main events in a story and then rate the events along some scale, such as excitement or impact on the character. Events are numbered, and these numbers are placed along a horizontal axis, as in Example 4.10. The rating for each event is plotted along the vertical axis. Lines are drawn between each point, thus creating a line graph. Johnson and Louis suggest that when students rate events in terms of their excitement, they use the following scale: "calm," "very interesting," "exciting," "WOW!"

Example 4.10

- **Title:** *Number the Stars*
- **Author:** Lois Lowry
- **Summary:** This is the story of one family's efforts to help save Danish Jews from the Nazis.

(continued)

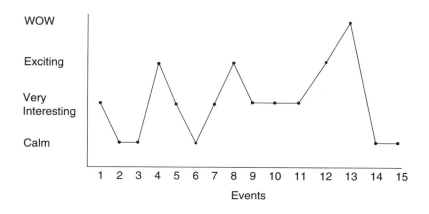

Events

1. Running home from school, Ellen, Annemarie, and Kirsti are stopped by German soldiers.

2. Peter visits after curfew and tells the family that Germans are ordering stores run by Jews closed.

3. Ellen comes to stay with the Johansens when her parents flee.

4. The soldiers search the Johansen apartment for the Rosen family. They challenge Ellen because of her dark hair.

5. Mrs. Johansen, Annemarie, Ellen, and Kirsti travel to Uncle Henrik's.

6. The girls play at Uncle Henrik's.

7. "Aunt Bertie's" loved ones gather around her casket.

8. The soldiers interrupt the gathering.

9. Peter organizes the Jews to head to the boat.

10. Mrs. Johansen leaves with the Rosens.

11. Annemarie sees her mother on the ground and helps her to the house.

12. Annemarie races through the woods to deliver the envelope to Henrik.

13. Annemarie is stopped and questioned by soldiers. They discover the package.

14. Uncle Henrik explains the Resistance and the handkerchief to Annemarie.

15. The war ends. Annemarie learns the truth about Lise's death.

An alternative to a line graph is a cut-and-paste grid. Students write each event from the story on a separate piece of paper. These may be illustrated. Students then paste these sheets higher or lower on a large butcher paper grid, depending upon the ratings they give. The key events and ratings shown in the line graph in Example 4.10 are depicted in the cut-and-paste format in Example 4.11.

Children can work individually or they can collaborate in small groups on plot profiles, coming to consensus on story events and ratings. If other individuals or groups of students are reading the same book, plot profiles can be compared. Teachers should expect differences between individual or group selections of key events and ratings.

Example 4.11 _____

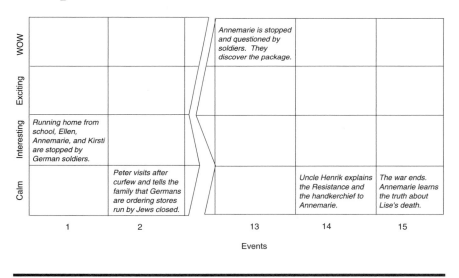

WOW				Annemarie is stopped and questioned by soldiers. They discover the package.		
Exciting						
Interesting	Running home from school, Ellen, Annemarie, and Kirsti are stopped by German soldiers.					
Calm		Peter visits after curfew and tells the family that Germans are ordering stores run by Jews closed.			Uncle Henrik explains the Resistance and the handkerchief to Annemarie.	The war ends. Annemarie learns the truth about Lise's death.
	1	2		13	14	15

Events

WORLD WHEELS

A world wheel may be used to help students organize information from books that present variations on experiences that people around the world share. For instance, in *Throw Your Tooth on the Roof*, by Selby B. Beeler, tooth traditions around the world are described. In Argentina, when young children lose a baby tooth, it is put into a glass of water. During the night, a little mouse drinks the water, takes the tooth, and leaves some coins or candy in the glass. In Costa Rica, the tooth is plated with gold and made into an earring. In *This Is the Way We Go to School*, by Edith Baer, readers meet children traveling to their respective schools in more than twenty locations throughout the world. Children are seen riding their bikes to school in China, taking the elevated rail transit in

Chicago, Illinois, and traveling by train in Kenya. In *Bread Bread Bread*, by Ann Morris, readers are introduced to many different kinds of bread that are enjoyed in different ways around the world. In *This Is My House*, by Arthur Dorros, readers learn about the similarities and differences among homes around the world, and in *Talking Walls*, by Margy Burns Knight, children are exposed to landmark walls around the world, including the Great Wall of China, the ancient walls of the Lascaux cave in France, the Wailing Wall in Jerusalem, the carved walls in Mahabalipuram, India, and the Berlin Wall.

World wheels help readers summarize the information in these books. In the examples below, students have included in their world wheel only some of the information included in the books. Students may choose information that they find most interesting, information related to countries they have studied, information related to countries represented in the classroom, or, in the case of the example that follows, information about hopscotch activities they would like to try. Of course, if the students wish to include all information offered by the text, they should not be discouraged— with some books the wheel will have many spokes!

Example 4.12 _____

- **Title:** *Hopscotch Around the World*
- **Author:** May D. Lankford
- **Grade Level:** 2–6
- **Summary:** The reader learns that hopscotch is an ancient game that is played in a variety of forms around the world. A brief narrative about each of 19 regions and detailed directions for 19 versions of the game are provided.

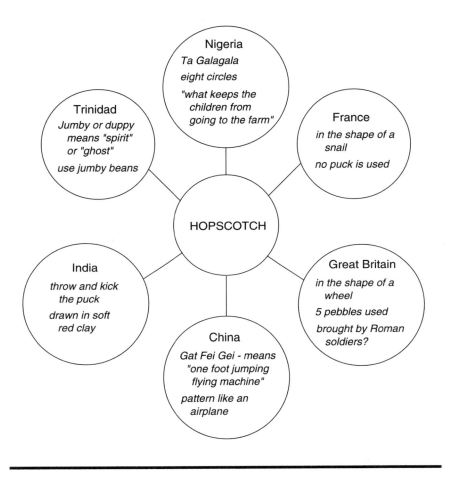

Example 4.13 _____

- **Title:** *Welcoming Babies*
- **Author:** Margy Burns Knight
- **Grade Level:** K–3
- **Summary:** "Every day, everywhere, babies are born. We have many ways to show them we are glad they came into the world." So begins this book that introduces readers to the many ways people of different cultures welcome newborns into the world.

(continued)

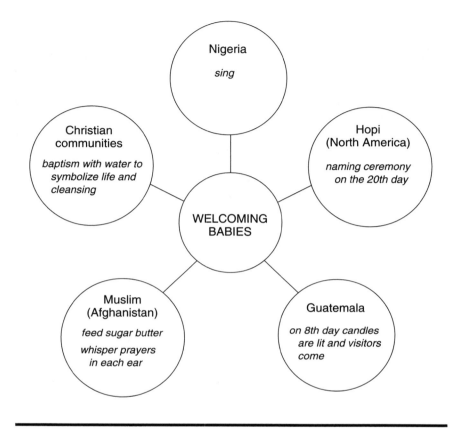

World wheels provide a vehicle for organizing information that students find in books that expose them to the diversity in the world, and at the same time help them understand what is common in the human experience. The strategy can serve as a stimulus for students' exploration of their own backgrounds and pique their interest in learning about the cultural heritage of others. Students could be encouraged to include an additional spoke in which they record their own personal experience. In Example 4.12 they could include "How I play hopscotch"; in Example 4.13 they could include "How I was welcomed into the world." Discussions with family would enrich this activity.

VENN DIAGRAMS

Venn diagrams offer a means for students to compare and contrast story elements (such as characters) in a book or to compare and contrast two or more books. Venn diagrams provide graphic representations of common and contrasting features. The teacher may introduce Venn diagrams by drawing two overlapping circles on the chalkboard. The circles represent the different elements or different books. Where the circles overlap, attributes that two elements have in common or content shared by two books is recorded. In the non-overlapping portions of the circles, attributes that are unique to each element or book are recorded. Example 4.14 displays a Venn diagram comparing and contrasting fruit bats and birds from the book *Stellaluna*.

Example 4.14 _____

- **Title:** *Stellaluna*
- **Author:** Janell Cannon
- **Grade Level:** K–3
- **Summary:** A fruit bat is cared for by a family of birds after falling from its mother's grasp while fleeing an owl. The bat and birds find that even though they are different, they are alike.

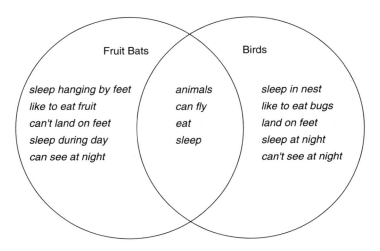

Fruit Bats	animals	Birds
sleep hanging by feet	can fly	sleep in nest
like to eat fruit	eat	like to eat bugs
can't land on feet	sleep	land on feet
sleep during day		sleep at night
can see at night		can't see at night

Comparisons can be made across books. For instance, the perspectives and actions of Johnny in *Johnny Tremain*, by Esther Forbes, can be compared and contrasted with those of Tim in *My Brother Sam Is Dead*, by James Lincoln Collier and Christopher Collier. Each of these characters is a boy who lives during the time of the American Revolution. *Adam of the Road*, by Elizabeth Janet Gray can be compared to *The Door in the Wall*, by Marguerite de Angeli. Each of these books details the experiences of a boy growing up during the Middle Ages.

Example 4.15 _____

- **Titles:** *Dandelions* (Eve Bunting)
  Going West (Jean Van Leeuwen)
- **Grade Level:** 2–4
- **Summary:** Each of these books describes the experiences of a family that travels by covered wagon to build a new home out west.

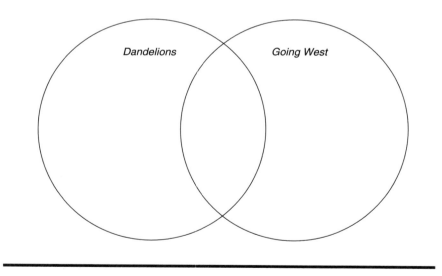

An interesting variation on this activity is to have students use Venn diagrams to compare themselves to a character. In Example 4.16, students can compare their lifestyles to that of a young boy whose people have a Stone Age way of life.

Example 4.16 _____

- **Title:** *Lobo of the Tasaday*
- **Author:** John Nance
- **Grade Level:** 2–5
- **Summary:** Lobo is a young member of the Tasaday, a group of people who live in a rain forest on an island in the southern Philippines. The author tells the true story of their Stone Age lifestyle and their discovery by the modern world in 1971.

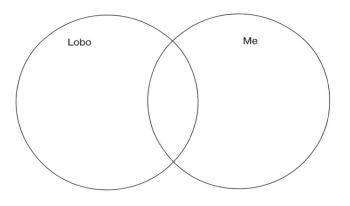

BOOK CHARTS

Book charts provide a structure for making comparisons among books, thus moving the students beyond "local reading" (Wolf in Hartman & Hartman, 1993)—a narrow focus on individual works of literature with little or no effort to make connections across texts. Through the use of book charts, students can discover patterns in literature, identify conventions in different genres of literature, and come to recognize the universality of specific themes. Their roles as readers are expanded beyond "the boundaries of a single text" (Hartman & Hartman, p. 202). Students can compare and contrast characters' experiences and their responses to those experiences, analyze similarities and differences in plots, and examine authors' strategies for developing common themes.

If students have read or listened to *In the Year of the Boar and Jackie Robinson* by Bette Lord, *Dragonwings* by Laurence Yep, and

Journey to America by Sonia Levitin, then a book chart that focuses on the theme "immigrants" may be useful for recording information and making comparisons. Several categories may be listed on a chart. In the immigrant example, categories might include "book," "author," "character," "native country," "positive experiences," and "negative experiences." Upon the completion of each book, information is written in the chart. Book charts may be developed by individual students or small groups, or large class charts may be generated. Class charts may be written on butcher paper and pinned to a bulletin board to remain in view for weeks or even months, depending upon the number of books included on the chart. Completed book charts will prove to be useful guides for students as they write analytical papers or their own stories on the same theme.

Example 4.17

- **Grade Level:** 3–6
- **Theme:** Lessons

Book Chart

Title	Author	Character	Lesson
The War with Grandpa	*Robert K. Smith*	*Peter*	*War isn't fun. War doesn't solve problems.*
The Hundred Dresses	*Eleanor Estes*	*Maddie*	*Don't just stand by when others are doing cruel things.*
Eyes of the Dragon	*Margaret Leaf*	*The magistrate*	*It is important to keep your word.*

The Cay by Theodore Taylor, *Call of the Wild* by Jack London, and *The Pinballs* by Betsy Byars, appropriate for grades 6 and up, could be used on a chart focusing on "obstacles," since the main characters in each of these books must overcome obstacles such as prejudice, physical disabilities, unforeseen circumstances, and abusive relationships in order to survive (psychologically or physically). A "survival" theme could be the focus of a book chart that includes *The Sign of the Beaver* by Elizabeth George Speare, *Island of the Blue Dolphins* by Scott O'Dell, *Hatchet* by Gary Paulsen, and *Julie of the Wolves* by Jean Craighead George. In each of these books, the protagonist is stranded alone somewhere and must find strength from within to survive the elements. Categories on the book chart might include author, title, reason the protagonist is alone, challenges faced, and outcome.

Book charts are also appropriate for primary-grade students. Three books that have a character who makes wishes are *Sylvester and the Magic Pebble* by William Steig, *The Magic Fish* by Freya Littledale, and *The Three Wishes* by M. Jean Craig. Students may identify the title of the book, the author, and the wishes. The consequences of the wishes could be discussed and students could share wishes they themselves might make. With younger children, the teacher may play a greater role in facilitating discussions and recording information.

Western (1980) describes a book chart in which students compare the characters, setting, problem, and ending of three versions of *Jack and the Beanstalk* and analyze their similarities and differ-

ences. A framework for this type of book chart using three versions
of the Cinderella story is provided in Example 4.18.

Example 4.18 _____

- **Titles:** *Yeh-Shen: A Cinderella Story from China* (Ai-Ling Louie)
  Moss Gown (William H. Hooks)
  The Egyptian Cinderella (Shirley Climo)
- **Grade Level:** 2–5

Book Chart
Version

	Yeh-Shen	Moss Gown	The Egyptian Cinderella	Similarities	Differences	Conclusions
Characters						
Setting						
Problem						
Ending						

Another type of book chart is the inquiry chart, or I-chart
(Hoffman, 1992). As can be seen in Example 4.19, students record
questions they have about a topic and anything they already know
related to the questions. Then the students consult a variety of

sources and record their findings on the chart. At the bottom of the chart, students summarize information. Students must compare information across texts and sometimes reconcile conflicting data in order to complete their summaries.

Example 4.19

- **Grade Level:** 2–4

I-Chart

Topic: Frogs	What is their habitat?	What do they eat?	What preys on them?	Other Interesting Facts	New Questions
What we know					
It's a Frog's Life (Steve Parker)					
Very First Things to Know about Frogs (Patricia Grossman)					
The Frog (Paul Starosta)					
Frogs (Gail Gibbons)					
Summary					

CONCLUSION

Postreading activities are useful for enhancing students' comprehension of, personal response to, and appreciation for literature. Polar opposites and literary report cards provide interesting and motivating formats for thinking about and analyzing characters. Quotation shares allow all students to share and respond to selections in the literature that they find compelling. Venn diagrams, world wheels, book charts, and plot organizers offer means for summarizing, organizing, and integrating information. Each of these seven types of postreading activities provides an opportunity for students to listen, speak, read, and write and encourages critical thinking. Most are open-ended and allow students to bring their individuality to the activity. Hopefully, teachers will take the time to engage students in postreading activities such as these that encourage students to continue to think about characters, issues, and events in and across books after they have read them.

REFERENCES

Baer, E. (1990). *This is the way we go to school.* New York: Scholastic.

Banks, L. (1982). *The Indian in the cupboard.* New York: Avon.

Beck, I. (1992). *Five little ducks.* New York: The Trumpet Club.

Beeler, S. B. (1998). *Throw your tooth on the roof: Tooth traditions from around the world.* Boston: Houghton Mifflin.

Bunting, E. (1995). *Dandelions.* San Diego, CA: Harcourt Brace.

Byars, B. (1977). *The pinballs.* New York: Harper & Row.

Cannon, J. (1993). *Stellaluna.* San Diego, CA: Harcourt Brace.

Christelow, E. (1989). *Five little monkeys jumping on the bed.* New York: Clarion.

Climo, S. (1989). *The Egyptian Cinderella.* New York: Thomas Y. Crowell.

Collier, J. L., & Collier, C. (1974). *My brother Sam is dead.* New York: Four Winds.

Craig, M. J. (1968). *The three wishes.* New York: Scholastic.

Curtis, C. P. (1995). *The Watsons go to Birmingham—1963.* New York: Bantam Doubleday Dell.

de Angeli, M. (1949). *The door in the wall.* New York: Scholastic.

DeGroff, L., & Galda, L. (1992) Responding to literature: Activities for exploring books. In B. Cullinan (Ed.), *Invitation to read: More children's literature in the reading program.* Newark, DE: International Reading Association.

Dorros, A. (1992). *This is my house.* New York: Scholastic.

Estes, E. (1974). *The hundred dresses.* San Diego, CA: Harcourt Brace Jovanovich.

Forbes, E. (1971). *Johnny Tremain.* New York: Dell.

Frost, R. (1959). *You come too.* New York: Holt, Rinehart, & Winston.

George, J. C. (1972). *Julie of the wolves.* New York: Harper & Row.

Gibbons, G. (1993). *Frogs.* New York: Holiday House.

Gray, E. J. (1942). *Adam of the road.* New York: Puffin.

Grossman, P. (1999). *Very first things to know about frogs.* New York: Workman.

Hartman, D. K., & Hartman, J. A. (1993). Reading across texts: Expanding the role of the reader. *The Reading Teacher, 47,* 202–211.

Heilbroner, J. (1962). *This is the house where Jack lives.* New York: Harper & Row.

Hoffman, J. V. (1992). Critical reading/thinking across the curriculum. Using I-charts to support learning. *Language Arts, 69,* 121–127.

Hooks, W. (1987). *Moss gown.* New York: Clarion Books.

Johnson, T., & Louis, D. (1987). *Literacy through literature.* Portsmouth, NH: Heinemann.

Konigsburg, E. L. (1974). *From the mixed-up files of Mrs. Basil E. Frankweiler.* New York: Dell.

Knight, M. B. (1992). *Talking walls.* Gardiner, ME: Tilbury House.

Knight, M. B. (1994). *Welcoming babies.* Gardiner, ME: Tilbury House.

Lankford, M. D. (1992). *Hopscotch around the world.* New York: Morrow Junior Books.

Leaf, M. (1967). *The story of Ferdinand.* New York: Scholastic.

Leaf, M. (1987). *Eyes of the dragon.* New York: Lothrop, Lee & Shepard.

Levitin, S. (1971). *Journey to America.* New York: Atheneum.

Littledale, F. (1986). *The magic fish.* New York: Scholastic.

London, J. (1974). *Call of the wild.* New York: Simon & Schuster.

Lord, B. (1984). *In the year of the boar and Jackie Robinso*n. New York: Harper Junior Books.

Louie, A. L. (1982). *Yeh-Shen: A Cinderella story from China.* New York: Philomel.

Lowry, L. (1989). *Number the stars.* New York: Dell.

Morris, A. (1989). *Bread bread bread.* New York: Mulberry.

Nance, J. (1982). *Lobo of the Tasaday.* New York: Pantheon.

Numeroff, L. J. (1985). *If you give a mouse a cookie.* New York: Harper & Row.

O'Dell, S. (1960). *Island of the blue dolphins.* Boston: Houghton Mifflin.

Parker, S. (1999). *It's a frog's life.* Pleasantville, NY: Reader's Digest Children's Books.

Paulsen, G. (1987). *Hatchet.* New York: The Trumpet Club.

Potter, B. (1989). *The tale of Peter Rabbit.* London: Penguin.

Sharmat, M. W. (1977). *Nate the great.* New York: Dell.

Smith, R. (1984). *The war with Grandpa.* New York: Delacorte.

Speare, E. G. (1983). *The sign of the beaver.* Boston: Houghton Mifflin.

Starosta, P. (1996). *The frog.* Watertown, MA: Charlesbridge.

Steig, W. (1969). *Sylvester and the magic pebble.* New York: Simon & Schuster.

Taylor, T. (1970). *The cay.* New York: Avon.

Tompkins, G. E. (1997). *Literacy for the 21st century.* Upper Saddle River, NJ: Merrill.

Van Leeuwen, J. (1992). *Going West.* New York: Puffin.

Western, L. (1980). A comparative study of literature through folk tale variants. *Language Arts, 57,* 395–402.

Wood, A. (1984). *The napping house.* San Diego, CA: Harcourt Brace Jovanovich.

Yep, L. (1975). *Dragonwings.* New York: Harper Junior Books.

CHAPTER FIVE

Bookmaking _____

Bookmaking

Purposes

- To motivate children to read and write
- To stimulate creativity
- To provide a means for sharing students' writing
- To promote problem solving and decision making
- To promote comprehension and language development

Activities

- Pop-up books
- Accordion books
- Fold-up books
- Upside-down books
- Retelling picture books

Publishing student books in the classroom is a natural extension of reading books. Literature provides an excellent model for writing, and students should have many opportunities to write in reponse to good books. Bookmaking moves children toward an understanding of writing and reading as exciting, personally meaningful, communicative activities. Students gain a greater sense of audience (Bromley, 1988; Holdaway, 1979), and they are more likely to make spontaneous revisions in their writing (DeFord, 1984) when they engage in bookmaking. Bookmaking encourages students to reread their own writing and that of their classmates often.

When developing books as a response to literature, students may summarize the story or information from the original work or they may borrow aspects of the author's literary structure to create their own book. (Lancia, 1997).

A book that follows a repetitious pattern, such as *Over in the Meadow*, retold by John Langstaff, provides a scaffold for students' writing. In this book, the author describes ten meadow animals. The rhythm and use of rhyme remain the same throughout the story. The students may change the setting and the animals in the story to create their own books, while maintaining the author's patterns. For example, they may write *Over in the Forest* or *Over in the Desert*. This will be especially interesting if the students are studying habitats in science. Another option is to have students continue with the author's setting and add an eleventh meadow animal, a twelfth, and so on.

The repetition in *The Little Red Hen*, by Vera Southgate, is also easily modeled. Students select an activity other than the planting of seeds, such as the baking of cupcakes, and identify and list the steps required in performing that activity. Then they use the language and structure of *The Little Red Hen*, substituting the cupcake activity. In addition, the students might provide different characters, such as relatives or friends. Each responds with "Not I," following the pattern established by the author.

The House That Jack Built, by David Cutts, and *I Know an Old Lady*, by Rose Bonne, both of which follow cumulative patterns, are excellent choices for modeling, as are books such as *Chicken Soup with Rice*, by Maurice Sendak, and *The Very Hungry Caterpillar*, by Eric Carle, which follow sequence patterns.

Many works of nonfiction, too, provide a structure that can be borrowed. *I Didn't Know That Crocodiles Yawn to Keep Cool*, by Kate Petty, begins each page with the phrase "I didn't know that . . ." Individuals or groups of students can select another topic (e.g., tigers, hurricanes, molecules) and present information about it using the same structure. Patricia Grossman's *Very First Things to Know about Frogs* follows a number pattern. David Schwartz's *G Is for Googol: A Math Alphabet Book* follows an alphabet pattern.

Student books should be placed in a classroom library or in any location where they are visible and accessible. Classroom books are intended to be handled and read over and over again. Sharing need not be restricted to the immediate classroom. Students may read their books to children in other classrooms or take one home overnight and share it with family members.

Many student-created books contain a "reader-response" page. This page typically is placed at the end of the book and invites written comments from readers, including other students, classroom guests, the principal, parents, and siblings. What a wonderful opportunity for authors to experience an audience and receive feedback!

In the remainder of this chapter, we provide directions for constructing *pop-up books, accordion books, fold-up books, upsidedown books*, and *retelling picture books*. Each of these book types may be used as a vehicle for summarizing a work of literature or modeling the language and structure of a selection. Each may be developed and constructed by individuals or groups.

The purposes of engaging children in bookmaking activities are as follows:

- To motivate children to read and write
- To stimulate creativity
- To provide a means for sharing
- To promote problem solving and decision making
- To promote comprehension and language development

POP-UP BOOKS

Pop-up books are fun and easy to construct. Children love the three-dimensional nature of these books, and parents are always impressed with their child's product. To make each page of the book, follow these simple directions:

1. Fold a piece of paper in half. Construction paper provides the best thickness and support for the pop-up pictures, but copy paper will do. Make two cuts of equal length about one inch apart into the creased edge of the paper.

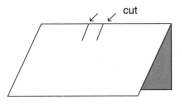

2. Open the paper so the two halves form a right angle. Pull the cut section through and fold it inward.

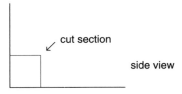

3. Paste a picture onto the cut section as shown.

You will probably want to have your students draw background pictures prior to pasting the pop-ups onto the page. The narrative also should be written on the paper prior to pasting and is typically on the bottom half of the paper.

Several pop-up figures may be placed on one page. Their size can vary by making shorter or longer cuts and by making the cuts closer together or farther apart. Each page should be constructed separately.

The Three Bears

4. Fold each paper back in half, stack the pages in order, and glue.

ACCORDION BOOKS

Accordion books are a wonderful activity for cooperative learning groups and provide an excellent opportunity for problem solving. First, the students must divide a reading selection into meaningful sections. The number of sections will depend partly on the age of the students. Once the group determines the sections, each student illustrates and writes a brief narrative for one of the sections on a 9-by-12-inch piece of tagboard. The boards are then lined up end to end and taped or tied together in sequence. Books may stand freely on counters accordion-style or be folded for storage.

To ensure a cohesive product, group members should thoroughly discuss and agree upon narration and illustrations prior to making individual assignments. If students do not discuss details, they run the risk of having a final product that lacks continuity and is clumsy. For example, one page may be written in the present tense and the next in the past tense, or the protagonist may be blond on one page and brunette on the next.

It is always interesting to have groups share their completed books. Students will notice that each group chose to summarize and illustrate the selection differently. Groups may vary in the events they chose to depict and in their illustrations.

Younger children may need to be guided through the summarization of the selection and the assignment of individual sections.

FOLD-UP BOOKS

Students can create a book that opens like a traditional book by folding and cutting a single sheet of paper. The size of the book will depend upon the size of the paper used. Some students will enjoy making Big Books (Holdaway, 1979) using butcher paper, and others will prefer to make miniatures using an $8\frac{1}{2}$-by-11-inch piece of paper. Directions must be followed carefully.

1. Fold a rectangular piece of paper into eighths as shown, pressing firmly on the creases. Open the paper, then refold the opposite direction on the same folds, again creasing firmly.

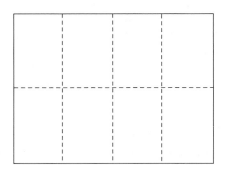

2. Fold the paper in half and cut on the center line as shown.

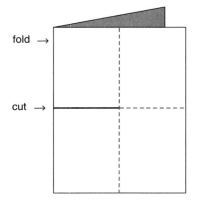

3. Open the paper. Lift points *a* and *c*, pulling them upward and away from each other so that points *b* and *d* come together. This will be difficult if folds are not well creased.

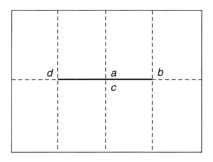

Your paper should look like this from the top:

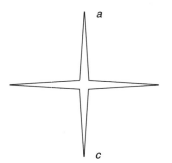

4. Bring all flaps together to form the book. Crease all folds.

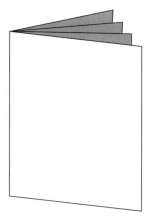

5. Students may then summarize the story and illustrate each page.

UPSIDE-DOWN BOOKS

This type of book is most useful when contrasting ideas are discussed or suggested by a piece of literature. One idea may be written on one side of a piece of paper, and the contrasting idea may be written upside down on the reverse side. For example, students may write about both a horrible, terrible day and a wonderful, delightful day after reading the story *Alexander and the Terrible, Horrible, No Good, Very Bad Day*, by Judith Viorst. Use the following format:

1. Each student completes a prompt such as "It was a horrible, terrible, no good, very bad day when . . . ." on a piece of paper and illustrates it.

2. Upside down and on the reverse side of the paper, each student completes and illustrates a second prompt such as "It was a wonderful, delightful, marvelous, fantastic day when . . . ." (Students may complete the second picture and narration on a separate piece of paper. Papers may subsequently be pasted on a sheet of construction paper, one on the front and one upside down on the back.)

3. All student papers are collected and stacked together, the same side up. In other words, all the "horrible day" sentences and illustrations are facing up, and all the "wonderful day" sentences and illustrations are facing down (and are upside down). An appropriate title page should be put on the front and the back. Bind the pages with staples, ribbons, brads, or whatever is available. When the book is read in one direction, it is the story of very bad days. When the book is turned over and upside down, it is the story of wonderful days.

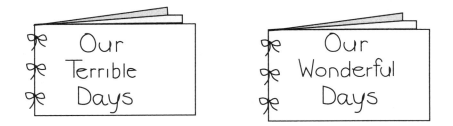

Information recorded in a contrast chart can provide ideas for an upside-down book. For example, the advantages and disadvantages of being two inches tall were listed in a contrast chart for *Stuart Little*, by E. B. White, in Chapter Two of this book. Students may create an upside-down book based on this chart with one side of the paper illustrating "A good thing about being two inches tall is . . . ." and the reverse side of the paper illustrating "A bad thing about being two inches tall is . . . ."

RETELLING PICTURE BOOKS

Retelling picture books allow students to retell stories with the help of attached characters that can be moved on and off the pages of a book. First, settings are identified and illustrations are drawn, painted, or cut and pasted onto pieces of paper that become the pages of the book. A title page is created that includes a pocket in which characters may be stored. The pages are then bound together by any means.

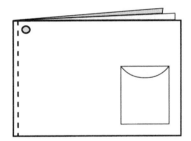

Next, characters are drawn onto tagboard and cut out. A hole is punched in each character, and a ribbon is tied through the hole. The other end of the ribbon is tied through a hole punched in the upper left-hand corner of the book. The ribbons must be long enough so that the students can move the characters freely. Three feet is a good length.

Students may then move the characters onto each page of the book as they retell the story.

One student teacher constructed a retelling picture book with a class of kindergarteners. She had each of her students make the following illustrations for *Goldilocks and the Three Bears*, by Lorinda Bryan Cauley, on 12-by-18-inch pieces of construction paper:

Page 1: the bears' house in the middle of a forest

Page 2: three bowls of porridge with the words "Papa," "Mama," and "Baby" written on them

Page 3: three chairs and a stairway

Page 4: three beds

After a title page was created and the pages were bound together, each student drew a picture of Goldilocks on tagboard and cut it out. Each also drew the three bears, cut them out, and pasted them together side by side so they could be moved about as a single entity. Goldilocks and the bears were then connected by ribbons to a corner of the book as just described.

When the children retold the story, they removed the characters from the pocket on the title page, opened the first page of the book, and moved the appropriate characters onto the page. On page 1, the Bears were moved from the house into the forest to go for a walk. Goldilocks was moved onto the page to discover the bears' open house. On page 2, Goldilocks was moved from bowl to bowl before finding Baby Bear's porridge just right to eat. The students continued retelling the story while moving the characters from page to page.

A retelling picture book provides students with a structure for retelling a story, and the scenes serve as reminders for each part of the story. Retelling picture books are very motivational and serve as wonderful vehicles for language development. Furthermore,

this activity is adaptable to many grade levels. Older children may make books for younger children or may develop a retelling picture book for a section of a novel they are reading.

CONCLUSION

Constructing their own books in response to literature is a highly motivational activity that promotes children's comprehension and language development. In addition, it reinforces a view of reading and writing as acts of communication. It is one of the most meaningful literacy activities in which students of any age can engage, and at the same time it can be supportive of other areas of the curriculum.

REFERENCES

Bonne, R. (1985). *I know an old lady*. New York: Scholastic.
Bromley, K. (1988). *Language arts: Exploring connections*. Boston: Allyn and Bacon.

Carle, E. (1987). *The very hungry caterpillar.* New York: Scholastic.

Cauley, L. B. (1981). *Goldilocks and the three bears.* New York: Putnam.

Cutts, D. (1979). *The house that Jack built.* Mahwah, NJ: Troll Associates.

DeFord, D. (1984). Classroom context for literacy learning. In T. Raphael (Ed.), *The context of school-based literacy* (pp. 163–180). New York: Random House.

Grossman, P. (1999). *Very first things to know about frogs.* New York: Workman.

Holdaway, D. (1979). *The foundations of literacy.* Exeter, NH: Heinemann.

Lancia, P. J. (1997). Literary borrowing: The effects of literature on children's writing. *The Reading Teacher, 50,* 470–475.

Langstaff, J. (1973). *Over in the meadow.* New York: Harcourt Brace Jovanovich.

Petty, K. (1998). *I didn't know that crocodiles yawn to keep cool.* Brookfield, CT: Copper Beech.

Schwartz, D. M. (1998). *G is for googol: A Math alphabet book.* Berkeley, CA; Tricycle.

Sendak, M. (1986). *Chicken soup with rice.* New York: Scholastic.

Southgate, V. (1966). *The little red hen.* Loughborough, England: Wills & Hepworth.

Viorst, J. (1976). *Alexander and the terrible, horrible, no good, very bad day.* New York: Macmillan.

White, E. B. (1973). *Stuart Little.* New York: Harper & Row.

Afterword

We hope that teachers will find the activities described in this book useful for promoting meaningful interactions with literature and inspiring a love of reading in their students. Before teachers incorporate these activities into their literature programs, however, we would like to issue a few cautions.

First, it is important that teachers know their students and make instructional decisions based upon students' interests and needs. Activities that are appropriate for some individuals may be less valuable for others. For example, some students may have considerable background knowledge on a particular topic and so will need less time devoted to building background knowledge prior to interacting with the selection. Other students may have little background knowledge on the topic and will profit from participation in a number of prereading activities.

Second, teachers should not be surprised if students do not engage in a grand conversation the first time an activity is attempted. Many children have experienced only gentle (or not so gentle!) inquisitions in school settings. They have learned that there is only one correct answer, that the most verbal students will provide it, or that if they wait long enough the teacher will provide it. This is especially true of older students who have had more time to learn these lessons. Given these expectations, it is not likely that all students will respond enthusiastically to the activities at first. Teachers must attempt the activities several times before achieving participation from everyone, while at the same time building trust and new expectations in their students.

Third, these activities should not be used as worksheets that are to be completed independently and collected for a grade. They are intended to arouse curiosity, activate background knowledge, focus attention on themes or language, promote comprehension, encourage reflection on issues or events encountered in books, and help students find literature selections personally meaningful. Few independently completed worksheets achieve these goals. They can be achieved, however, through meaningful interaction among students and with the teacher.

Fourth, literature activities should not be overused. We know one teacher who implemented several prereading activities before every chapter of a novel. We were not surprised when she told us that her students disliked the novel, and lost enthusiasm for the activities. Anything can be overdone. Teachers should exercise reason when using literature activities before, during, and after reading. Sometimes it is most appropriate to use none at all.

Finally, teachers should provide students with many opportunities to read and listen to literature in the classroom throughout the day and in many contexts. These opportunities, along with an extensive classroom library, will go a long way toward promoting a love of reading.

APPENDIX A

Resources for Teachers

JOURNALS AND MAGAZINES

Bookbird: World of Children's Books
International Board of Books for Young People (IBBY)
P.O. Box 807
Highland Park, IL 60035-0807
http://www.ibby.org

Booklist and BookLinks
American Library Association
50 E. Huron Street
Chicago, IL 60611
(800) 545-2433
http://www.ala.org

Bulletin of the Center for Children's Book
University of Illinois Press
1325 S. Oak Street
Champaign, IL 61820
(217) 244-0626

The Horn Book Magazine
56 Roland St., Suite 200
Boston, MA 02129
(800) 325-1170
http://www.hbook.com

Kirkus Reviews
200 Park Avenue South
New York, NY 10003-1543
(212) 777-4554

Language Arts and
    Journal of Children's Literature
National Council of Teachers of English
1111 W. Kenyon Road
Urbana, IL 61801-1096
(800) 369-6283
http://www.ncte.org

The New Advocate
Christopher-Gordon Publishers, Inc.
480 Washington Street
Norwood, MA 02062
(508) 543-8729

The Reading Teacher and
    Journal of Adolescent and Adult Literacy
International Reading Association
800 Barksdale Road.
P.O. Box 8139
Newark, DE 19714-8139
(302) 731-1600
http://www.reading.org

School Library Journal
P.O. Box 57559
Boulder, CO 80322
(800) 456-9409
http://www.slj.com

Science and Children
National Science Teachers Association
1840 Wilson Blvd.
Arlington, VA 22201
www.nsta.org

WEB SITES

American Library Association
www.ala.org/alsc/newbery.html
Provides information about the Newbery Medal and lists of award winners

www.ala.org/alsc/caldecott.html
Provides information about the Caldecott Medal and lists of award winners

www.ala.org/srrt/csking/
Provides information about the Coretta Scott King Award and lists of award winners

Bibliofind
http://www.bibliofind.com
Locates out-of-print, hard-to-find, and rare books

Bookfinder
http://www.bookfinder.com
Locates new and used books.

The Children's Literature Web Guide
http://www.acs.ucalgary.ca/~dkbrown/index.html
Provides information about Internet resources related to books for children and adults

The Horn Book
www.hbook.com
Go to Horn Book Awards for lists of award-winning books.

National Council of Teachers of English
www.ncte.org
Provides information about the Orbis Pictus Award and list of award winners.

National Science Teachers Assocation
www.nsta.org/pubs/sc/ostblist.asp
Provides lists of Outstanding Science Trade Books for Children

APPENDIX B

Award-Winning Literature ——————

THE CALDECOTT MEDAL AND HONOR AWARDS

The Caldecott Medal, first awarded in 1938, is presented annually to the illustrator of the most distinguished picture book published in the United States. The award is named after Randolph Caldecott, a British illustrator, and is given by the Children's Services Division of the American Library Association.

1938 **Title:** *Animals of the Bible*
   Author: Helen Dean Fish
   Illustrator: Dorothy P. Lathrop
   Publisher: Frederick A. Stokes

   Honor Books: *Seven Simeons: A Russian Tale* by Boris Artzybasheff, Viking; *Four and Twenty Blackbirds: Nursery Rhymes of Yesterday Recalled for Children of Today* by Helen Dean Fish, illustrated by Robert Lawson, Frederick A. Stokes

1939 **Title:** *Mei Li*
   Author: Thomas Handforth
   Publisher: Doubleday, Doran

   Honor Books: *The Forest Pool* by Laura Adams Armer, Longmans, Green; *Wee Gillis* by Munro Leaf, illustrated by Robert Lawson, Viking; *Snow White and the Seven Dwarfs* by Wanda Gag, Coward-McCann; *Barkis* by Clare Newberry, Harper and Brothers; *Andy and the Lion: A Tale of Kindness Remembered or the Power of Gratitude* by James Daugherty, Viking

1940 Title: *Abraham Lincoln*
Authors: Ingri and Edgar Parin D'Aulaire
Publisher: Doubleday, Doran

Honor Books: *Cock-a-Doodle Doo: The Story of a Little Red Rooster* by Berta and Elmer Hader, Macmillan; *Madeline* by Ludwig Bemelmans, Simon & Schuster; *The Ageless Story* by Lauren Ford, Dodd, Mead

1941 Title: *They Were Strong and Good*
Author: Robert Lawson
Publisher: Viking

Honor Book: *April's Kittens* by Clare Newberry, Harper and Brothers

1942 Title: *Make Way for Ducklings*
Author: Robert McCloskey
Publisher: Viking

Honor Books: *An American ABC* by Maud and Miska Petersham, Macmillan; *In My Mother's House* by Ann Nolan Clark, illustrated by Velino Herrera, Viking; *Paddle-to-the-Sea* by Holling C. Holling, Houghton Mifflin; *Nothing at All* by Wanda Gag, Coward-McCann

1943 Title: *The Little House*
Author: Virginia Lee Burton
Publisher: Houghton Mifflin

Honor Books: *Dash and Dart* by Mary and Conrad Buff, Viking; *Marshmallow* by Clare Newberry, Harper and Brothers

1944 Title: *Many Moons*
Author: James Thurber
Illustrator: Louis Slobodkin
Publisher: Harcourt Brace

Honor Books: *Small Rain: Verses from the Bible* selected by Jessie Orton Jones, illustrated by Elizabeth Orton Jones, Viking; *Pierre Pigeon* by Lee Kingman, illustrated by Arnold E. Bare, Houghton Mifflin; *The Mighty Hunter* by Berta and Elmer Hader, Macmillan; *A Child's Good Night Book* by Margaret Wise Brown, illustrated by Jean Charlot, W. R.

Scott; *Good-Luck Horse* by Chih-Yi Chan, illustrated by Plato Chan, Whittlesey

1945 Title: *Prayer for a Child*
Author: Rachel Field
Illustrator: Elizabeth Orton Jones
Publisher: Macmillan

Honor Books: *Mother Goose: Seventy-Seven Verses with Pictures* illustrated by Tasha Tudor, Henry Z. Walck; *In the Forest* by Marie Hall Ets, Viking; *Yonie Wondernose* by Marguerite de Angeli, Doubleday; *The Christmas Anna Angel* by Ruth Sawyer, illustrated by Kate Seredy, Viking

1946 Title: *The Rooster Crows* (traditional Mother Goose)
Illustrators: Maud and Miska Petersham
Publisher: Macmillan

Honor Books: *Little Lost Lamb* by Golden MacDonald, illustrated by Leonard Weisgard, Doubleday; *Sing Mother Goose* by Opal Wheeler, illustrated by Marjorie Torrey, E. P. Dutton; *My Mother Is the Most Beautiful Woman in the World* by Becky Reyher, illustrated by Ruth Gannett, Howell, Soskin; *You Can Write Chinese* by Kurt Wiese, Viking

1947 Title: *The Little Island*
Author: Golden MacDonald
Illustrator: Leonard Weisgard
Publisher: Doubleday

Honor Books: *Rain Drop Splash* by Alvin Tresselt, illustrated by Leonard Weisgard, Lothrop, Lee & Shepard; *Boats on the River* by Marjorie Flack, illustrated by Jay Hyde Barnum, Viking; *Timothy Turtle* by Al Graham, illustrated by Tony Palazzo, Robert Welch; *Pedro, the Angel of Olvera Street* by Leo Politi, Charles Scribner's Sons; *Sing in Praise: A Collection of the Best-Loved Hymns* by Opal Wheeler, illustrated by Marjorie Torrey, E. P. Dutton

1948 Title: *White Snow, Bright Snow*
Author: Alvin Tresselt
Illustrator: Roger Duvoisin
Publisher: Lothrop, Lee & Shepard

Honor Books: *Stone Soup: An Old Tale* by Marcia Brown, Charles Scribner's Sons; *McElligot's Pool* by Dr. Seuss, Random House; *Bambino the Clown* by George Schreiber, Viking; *Roger and the Fox* by Lavinia Davis, illustrated by Hildegard Woodward, Doubleday; *Song of Robin Hood* edited by Anne Malcolmson, illustrated by Virginia Lee Burton, Houghton Mifflin

1949 Title: *The Big Snow*
Authors: Betta and Elmer Hader
Publisher: Macmillan

Honor Books: *Blueberries for Sal* by Robert McCloskey, Viking; *All Around the Town* by Phyllis McGinley, illustrated by Helen Stone, J. B. Lippincott; *Juanita* by Leo Politi, Charles Scribner's Sons; *Fish in the Air* by Kurt Wiese, Viking

1950 Title: *Song of the Swallows*
Author: Leo Politi
Publisher: Charles Scribner's Sons

Honor Books: *America's Ethan Allen* by Stewart Holbrook, illustrated by Lynd Ward, Houghton Mifflin; *The Wild Birthday Cake* by Lavinia Davis, illustrated by Hildegard Woodward, Doubleday; *The Happy Day* by Ruth Krauss, illustrated by Marc Simont, Harper and Brothers; *Bartholomew and the Oobleck* by Dr. Seuss, Random; *Henry Fisherman* by Marcia Brown, Charles Scribner's Sons

1951 Title: *The Egg Tree*
Author: Katherine Milhous
Publisher: Charles Scribner's Sons

Honor Books: *Dick Whittington and His Cat* by Marcia Brown, Charles Scribner's Sons; *The Two Reds* by William Lipkind, illustrated by Nicholas Mordvinoff, Harcourt; *If I Ran the Zoo* by Dr. Seuss, Random House; *The Most Wonderful Doll in the World* by Phyllis McGinley, illustrated by Helen Stone, J. B. Lippincott; *T-Bone, the Baby Sitter* by Clare Newberry, Harper and Brothers

1952 Title: *Finders Keepers*
Author: William Lipkind
Illustrator: Nicholas Mordvinoff
Publisher: Harcourt

Honor Books: *Mr. T. W. Anthony Wood: The Story of a Cat and a Dog and a Mouse* by Marie Hall Ets, Viking; *Skipper John's Cook* by Marcia Brown, Charles Scribner's Sons; *All Falling Down* by Gene Zion, illustrated by Margaret Bloy Graham, Harper and Brothers; *Bear Party* by William Pene du Bois, Viking; *Feather Mountain* by Elizabeth Olds, Houghton Mifflin

1953 Title: *The Biggest Bear*
Author: Lynd Ward
Publisher: Houghton Mifflin

Honor Books: *Puss in Boots* by Charles Perrault, illustrated and translated by Marcia Brown, Charles Scribner's Sons; *One Morning in Maine* by Robert McCloskey, Viking; *Ape in a Cape: An Alphabet of Odd Animals* by Fritz Eichenberg, Harcourt; *The Storm Book* by Charlotte Zolotow, illustrated by Margaret Bloy Graham, Harper and Brothers; *Five Little Monkeys* by Juliet Kepes, Houghton Mifflin

1954 Title: *Madeline's Rescue*
Author: Ludwig Bemelmans
Publisher: Viking

Honor Books: *Journey Cake, Ho!* by Ruth Sawyer, illustrated by Robert McCloskey, Viking; *When Will the World Be Mine?* by Miriam Schlein, illustrated by Jean Charlot, W. R. Scott; *The Steadfast Tin Soldier* by Hans Christian Andersen, translated by M. R. James, illustrated by Marcia Brown, Charles Scribner's Sons; *A Very Special House* by Ruth Krauss, illustrated by Maurice Sendak, Harper and Brothers; *Green Eyes* by Abe Birnbaum, Capitol

1955 Title: *Cinderella, or the Little Glass Slipper*
Author: Charles Perrault
Translator: Marcia Brown
Illustrator: Marcia Brown
Publisher: Charles Scribner's Sons

Honor Books: *Book of Nursery and Mother Goose Rhymes*, illustrated by Marguerite de Angeli, Doubleday; *Wheel on the Chimney* by Margaret Wise Brown, illustrated by Tibor Gergely, J. B. Lippincott; *The Thanksgiving Story* by Alice Dalgliesh, illustrated by Helen Sewell, Charles Scribner's Sons

1956 Title: *Frog Went A-Courtin'*
Editor: John Langstaff
Illustrator: Feodor Rojankovsky
Publisher: Harcourt

Honor Books: *Play with Me* by Marie Hall Ets, Viking; *Crow Boy* by Taro Yashima, Viking

1957 Title: *A Tree Is Nice*
Author: Janice May Udry
Illustrator: Marc Simont
Publisher: Harper and Brothers

Honor Books: *Mr. Penny's Race Horse* by Marie Hall Ets, Viking; *1 Is One* by Tasha Tudor, Henry Z. Walck; *Anatole* by Eve Titus, illustrated by Paul Galdone, Whittlesey; *Gillespie and the Guards* by Benjamin Elkin, illustrated by James Daugherty, Viking; *Lion* by William Pene du Bois, Viking

1958 Title: *Time of Wonder*
Author: Robert McCloskey
Publisher: Viking

Honor Books: *Fly High, Fly Low* by Don Freeman, Viking; *Anatole and the Cat* by Eve Titus, illustrated by Paul Galdone, Whittlesey

1959 Title: *Chanticleer and the Fox* (adapted from Chaucer)
Illustrator: Barbara Cooney
Publisher: Thomas Y. Crowell

Honor Books: *The House That Jack Built: A Picture Book in Two Languages* by Antonio Frasconi, Harcourt Brace; *What Do You Say, Dear?* by Sesyle Joslin, illustrated by Maurice Sendak, W. R. Scott; *Umbrella* by Taro Yashima, Viking

1960 Title: *Nine Days to Christmas*
Authors: Marie Hall Ets and Aurora Labastida
Illustrator: Marie Hall Ets
Publisher: Viking

Honor Books: *Houses from the Sea* by Alice E. Goudey, illustrated by Adrienne Adams, Charles Scribner's Sons; *The Moon Jumpers* by Janice May Udry, illustrated by Maurice Sendak, Harper and Brothers

1961 Title: *Baboushka and the Three Kings*
      Author: Ruth Robbins
      Illustrator: Nicolas Sidjakov
      Publisher: Parnassus Imprints

Honor Book: *Inch by Inch* by Leo Lionni, Obolensky

1962 Title: *Once a Mouse . . .*
      Author: Marcia Brown
      Publisher: Charles Scribner's Sons

Honor Books: *The Fox Went out on a Chilly Night: An Old Song* by Peter Spier, Doubleday; *Little Bear's Visit* by Else Holmelund Minarik, illustrated by Maurice Sendak, Harper and Brothers; *The Day We Saw the Sun Come Up* by Alice E. Goudey, illustrated by Adrienne Adams, Charles Scribner's Sons

1963 Title: *The Snowy Day*
      Author: Ezra Jack Keats
      Publisher: Viking

Honor Books: *The Sun Is a Golden Earring* by Natalia M. Belting, illustrated by Bernarda Bryson, Holt, Rinehart, & Winston; *Mr. Rabbit and the Lovely Present* by Charlotte Zolotow, illustrated by Maurice Sendak, Harper & Row

1964 Title: *Where the Wild Things Are*
      Author: Maurice Sendak
      Publisher: Harper & Row

Honor Books: *Swimmy* by Leo Lionni, Pantheon; *All in the Morning Early* by Sorche Nic Leodhas, illustrated by Evaline Ness, Holt, Rinehart, & Winston; *Mother Goose and Nursery Rhymes* illustrated by Philip Reed, Atheneum

1965 Title: *May I Bring a Friend?*
      Author: Beatrice Schenk de Regniers
      Illustrator: Beni Montresor
      Publisher: Atheneum

Honor Books: *Rain Makes Applesauce* by Julian Scheer, illustrated by Marvin Bileck, Holiday House; *The Wave* by Margaret Hodges, illustrated by Blair Lent, Houghton Mifflin; *A Pocketful of Cricket* by Rebecca Caudill, illustrated by Evaline Ness, Holt, Rinehart, & Winston

1966 **Title:**   *Always Room for One More*
        Author: Sorche Nic Leodhas
        Illustrator: Nonny Hogrogian
        Publisher: Holt, Rinehart, & Winston

        Honor Books: *Hide and Seek Fog* by Alvin Tresselt, illustrated by Roger Duvoisin, Lothrop, Lee & Shepard; *Just Me* by Marie Hall Ets, Viking; *Tom Tit Tot* by Evaline Ness, Charles Scribner's Sons

1967 **Title:**   *Sam, Bangs & Moonshine*
        Author: Evaline Ness
        Publisher: Holt, Rinehart, & Winston

        Honor Book: *One Wide River to Cross* by Barbara Emberley, illustrated by Ed Emberley, Prentice-Hall

1968 **Title:**   *Drummer Hoff*
        Author: Barbara Emberley
        Illustrator: Ed Emberley
        Publisher: Prentice-Hall

        Honor Books: *Frederick* by Leo Lionni, Pantheon; *Seashore Story* by Taro Yashima, Viking; *The Emperor and the Kite* by Jane Yolen, illustrated by Ed Young, World

1969 **Title:**   *The Fool of the World and the Flying Ship*
        Author: Arthur Ransom
        Illustrator: Uri Shulevitz
        Publisher: Farrar, Straus & Giroux

        Honor Book: *Why the Sun and the Moon Live in the Sky: An African Folktale* by Elphinstone Dayrell, illustrated by Blair Lent, Houghton Mifflin

1970 **Title:**   *Sylvester and the Magic Pebble*
        Author: William Steig
        Publisher: Windmill/Simon & Schuster

        Honor Books: *Goggles!* by Ezra Jack Keats, Macmillan; *Alexander and the Wind-Up Mouse* by Leo Lionni, Pantheon; *Pop Corn and Ma Goodness* by Edna Mitchell Preston, illustrated by Robert Andrew Parker, Viking; *Thy Friend, Obadiah* by Brinton Turkle, Viking; *The Judge: An Untrue Tale* by Harve Zemach, illustrated by Margot Zemach, Farrar, Straus & Giroux

1971 **Title:**   *A Story, A Story*
         Author: Gail E. Haley
         Publisher: Atheneum

Honor Books: *The Angry Moon* by William Sleator, illustrated by Blair Lent, Little, Brown; *Frog and Toad Are Friends* by Arnold Lobel, Harper & Row; *In the Night Kitchen* by Maurice Sendak, Harper & Row

1972 **Title:**   *One Fine Day*
         Author: Nonny Hogrogian
         Publisher: Macmillan

Honor Books: *If All the Seas Were One Sea* by Janina Domanska, Macmillan; *Moja Means One: Swahili Counting Book* by Muriel Feelings, illustrated by Tom Feelings, Dial; *Hildilid's Night* by Cheli Duran Ryan, illustrated by Arnold Lobel, Macmillan

1973 **Title:**   *The Funny Little Woman*
         Retold by: Arlene Mosel
         Illustrator: Blair Lent
         Publisher: E. P. Dutton

Honor Books: *Anansi the Spider: A Tale from the Ashanti* adapted and illustrated by Gerald McDermott, Holt, Rinehart, & Winston; *Hosie's Alphabet* by Hosea, Tobias, and Lisa Baskin, illustrated by Leonard Baskin, Viking; *Snow White and the Seven Dwarfs* translated by Randall Jarrell, illustrated by Nancy Ekholm Burkert, Farrar, Straus & Giroux; *When Clay Sings* by Byrd Baylor, illustrated by Tom Bahti, Charles Scribner's Sons

1974 **Title:**   *Duffy and the Devil*
         Author: Harve Zemach
         Illustrator: Margot Zemach
         Publisher: Farrar, Straus & Giroux

Honor Books: *Three Jovial Huntsmen* by Susan Jeffers, Bradbury; *Cathedral: The Story of Its Construction* by David Macaulay, Houghton Mifflin

1975 **Title:**   *Arrow to the Sun*
         Adapted by: Gerald McDermott
         Illustrator: Gerald McDermott
         Publisher: Viking

Honor Book: *Jambo Means Hello: A Swahili Alphabet Book* by Muriel Feelings, illustrated by Tom Feelings, Dial

1976 Title: *Why Mosquitoes Buzz in People's Ears*
Retold by: Verna Aardema
Illustrators: Leo and Diane Dillon
Publisher: Dial

Honor Books: *The Desert Is Theirs* by Byrd Baylor, illustrated by Peter Parnall, Charles Scribner's Sons: *Strega Nona*, retold and illustrated by Tomie dePaola, Prentice-Hall

1977 Title: *Ashanti to Zulu: African Traditions*
Author: Margaret Musgrove
Illustrators: Leo and Diane Dillon
Publisher: Dial

Honor Books: *The Amazing Bone* by William Steig, Farrar, Straus & Giroux; *The Contest*, retold and illustrated by Nony Hogrogian, Greenwillow; *Fish for Supper* by M. B. Goffstein, Dial; *The Golem: A Jewish Legend* by Beverly Brodsky McDermott, J. B. Lippincott; *Hawk, I'm Your Brother* by Byrd Baylor, illustrated by Peter Parnall, Charles Scribner's Sons

1978 Title: *Noah's Ark*
Author: Peter Spier
Publisher: Doubleday

Honor Books: *Castle* by David Macaulay, Houghton Mifflin; *It Could Always Be Worse*, retold and illustrated by Margot Zemach, Farrar, Straus & Giroux

1979 Title: *The Girl Who Loved Wild Horses*
Author: Paul Goble
Publisher: Bradbury

Honor Books: *Freight Train* by Donald Crews, Greenwillow; *The Way to Start a Day* by Byrd Baylor, illustrated by Peter Parnall, Charles Scribner's Sons

1980 Title: *Ox-Cart Man*
Author: Donald Hall
Illustrator: Barbara Cooney
Publisher: Viking

Honor Books: *Ben's Trumpet* by Rachel Isadora, Greenwillow; *The Treasure* by Uri Shulevitz, Farrar, Straus & Giroux; *The Garden of Abdul Gasazi* by Chris Van Allsburg, Houghton Mifflin

1981 **Title:** *Fables*
Author: Arnold Lobel
Publisher: Harper & Row

Honor Books: *The Bremen-Town Musicians* by Ilse Plume, Doubleday; *The Grey Lady and the Strawberry Snatcher* by Molly Bang, Four Winds; *Mice Twice* by Joseph Low, Atheneum; *Truck* by Donald Crews, Greenwillow

1982 **Title:** *Jumanji*
Author: Chris Van Allsburg
Publisher: Houghton Mifflin

Honor Books: *A Visit to William Blake's Inn: Poems for Innocent and Experienced Travelers* by Nancy Willard, illustrated by Alice and Martin Provensen, Harcourt Brace Jovanovich; *Where the Buffaloes Begin* by Olaf Baker, illustrated by Stephen Gammell, F. Warne; *On Market Street* by Arnold Lobel, illustrated by Anita Lobel, Greenwillow; *Outside over There* by Maurice Sendak, Harper & Row

1983 **Title:** *Shadow*
Author: Blaise Cendrars
Illustrator: Marcia Brown
Publisher: Charles Scribner's Sons

Honor Books: *When I Was Young in the Mountains* by Cynthia Rylant, illustrated by Diane Goode, E. P. Dutton; *A Chair for My Mother* by Vera B. Williams, Morrow

1984 **Title:** *The Glorious Flight: Across the Channel with Louis Bleriot, July 25, 1909*
Authors: Alice and Martin Provensen
Publisher: Viking

Honor Books: *Ten, Nine, Eight* by Molly Bang, Greenwillow; *Little Red Riding Hood*, retold and illustrated by Trina Schart Hyman, Holiday House

1985 **Title:** *St. George and the Dragon*
Retold by: Margaret Hodges

Illustrator: Trina Schart Hyman
Publisher: Little, Brown

Honor Books: *Hansel and Gretel*, retold by Rika Lesser, illustrated by Paul O. Zelinsky, Dodd; *Have You Seen My Duckling?* by Nancy Tafuri, Greenwillow; *The Story of Jumping Mouse* by John Steptoe, Lothrop, Lee & Shepard

1986 Title: *The Polar Express*
Author: Chris Van Allsburg
Publisher: Houghton Mifflin

Honor Books: *King Bidgood's in the Bathtub* by Audrey Wood, illustrated by Don Wood, Harcourt Brace Jovanovich; *The Relatives Came* by Cynthia Rylant, illustrated by Stephen Gammell, Bradbury

1987 Title: *Hey, Al*
Author: Arthur Yorinks
Illustrator: Richard Egielski
Publisher: Farrar, Straus & Giroux

Honor Books: *Alphabatics* by Suse MacDonald, Bradbury; *Rumpelstiltskin*, retold and illustrated by Paul O. Zelinsky, E. P. Dutton; *The Village of Round and Square Houses* by Ann Grifalconi, Little, Brown

1988 Title: *Owl Moon*
Author: Jane Yolen
Illustrator: John Schoenherr
Publisher: Philomel

Honor Book: *Mufaro's Beautiful Daughters: An African Tale* by John Steptoe, Lothrop, Lee & Shepard

1989 Title: *Song and Dance Man*
Author: Karen Ackerman
Illustrator: Stephen Gammell
Publisher: Alfred A. Knopf

Honor Books: *The Boy of the Three-Year Nap* by Dianne Snyder, illustrated by Allen Say, Houghton Mifflin; *Free Fall* by David Wiesner, Lothrop, Lee & Shepard; *Goldilocks*, retold and illustrated by James Marshall, Dial; *Mirandy and Brother Wind* by Patricia C. McKissack, illustrated by Jerry Pinkney, Alfred A. Knopf

1990 Title: *Lon Po Po: A Red Riding Hood Story from China*
Author: Ed Young
Publisher: Philomel

Honor Books: *Bill Peet: An Autobiography* by Bill Peet, Houghton Mifflin; *Color Zoo* by Lois Ehlert, J. B. Lippincott; *Hershel and the Hanukkah Goblins* by Eric Kimmel, illustrated by Trina Schart Hyman, Holiday House; *The Talking Eggs* by Robert D. San Souci, illustrated by Jerry Pinkney, Dial

1991 Title: *Black and White*
Author: Davis Macaulay
Publisher: Houghton Mifflin

Honor Books: *"More More More," Said the Baby: 3 Love Stories* by Vera B. Williams, Greenwillow; *Puss in Boots* by Charles Perrault, translated by Malcolm Arthur, illustrated by Fred Marcellino, Farrar, Straus & Giroux

1992 Title: *Tuesday*
Author: David Weisner
Publisher: Clarion

Honor Book: *Tar Beach* by Faith Ringold, Crown

1993 Title: *Mirette on the High Wire*
Author: Emily Arnold McCully
Publisher: G. P. Putnam's Sons

Honor Books: *Stinky Cheese Man and Other Fairly Stupid Tales* by Jon Scieska, illustrated by Lane Smith, Viking; *Working Cotton* by Sherley Anne Williams, illustrated by Carol Byard, Harcourt Brace; *Seven Blind Mice* by Ed Young, Philomel

1994 Title: *Grandfather's Journey*
Author: Allen Say
Publisher: Houghton Mifflin

Honor Books: *Peppe the Lamplighter* by Elisa Barton, illustrated by Ted Lewin, Lothrop, Lee & Shepard; *In the Small, Small Pond* by Denise Fleming, Henry Holt; *Owen* by Kevin Henkes, Greenwillow; *Raven: A Trickster Tale from the Pacific Northwest* by Gerald McDermott, Harcourt Brace; *Yo! Yes?* by Chris Raschka, Orchard

1995 Title: *Smoky Night*
     Author: Eve Bunting
     Illustrator: David Diaz
     Publisher: Harcourt Brace

Honor Books: *John Henry* by Julius Lester, illustrated by Jerry Pickney, Dial; *Swamp Angel* by Paul Zelinsky, illustrated by Anne Issacs, E. P. Dutton; *Time Flies* by Eric Rohmann, Crown

1996 Title: *Officer Buckle and Gloria*
     Author: Peggy Rathmann
     Publisher: Putnam

Honor Books: *Alphabet City* by Stephen T. Johnston, Viking; *Zin! Zin! Zin! A Violin* by Lloyd Moss, illustrated by Marjorie Priceman, Simon & Schuster; *The Faithful Friend* by Robert San Souci, illustrated by Brian Pinkney, Simon & Schuster, *Tops & Bottoms* by Janet Stevens, Harcourt

1997 Title: *Golem*
     Author: David Wisniewski
     Publisher: Clarion

Honor Books: *Hush! A Thai Lullaby* by Minfong Ho, illustrated by Holly Meade, Orchard; *The Graphic Alphabet* by David Pelletier, Orchard; *The Paperboy* by Dav Pilkey, Orchard; *Starry Messenger* by Peter Sis, Farrar, Straus, & Giroux

1998 Title: *Rapunzel*
     Author: Paul O. Zelinksy
     Publisher: E. P. Dutton

Honor Books: *The Gardener* by Sarah Stewart, illustrated by David Small, Farrar, Straus & Giroux; *Harlem* by Walter Dean Myers, illustrated by Chrisopher Myers, Scholastic; *There Was an Old Lady Who Swallowed a Fly* by Simms Taback, Viking

1999 Title: *Snowflake Bentley*
     Author: Jaqueline Briggs Martin
     Illustrator: Mary Azarian
     Publisher: Houghton Mifflin

Honor Books: *Duke Ellington: The Piano Prince and the Orchestra* by Andrea David Pinkney, illustrated by Brian Pinkney, Hyperion; *No, David!* by David Shannon, Scholastic; *Snow* by Uri Shulevitz, Farrar, Straus & Giroux; *Tibet Through the Red Box* by Peter Sis, Farrar, Straus & Giroux

THE NEWBERY MEDAL AND HONOR AWARDS

The Newbery award, first presented in 1922, is given annually for the most distinguished contributions to children's literature published in the United States. The award is named after John Newbery, the first English publisher of books for children, and is given by the Children's Services Division of the American Library Association.

1922 **Title:** *The Story of Mankind*
Author: Hendrik Willem van Loon
Publisher: Boni & Liveright

Honor Books: *The Great Quest* by Charles Hawes, Little, Brown; *Cedric the Forester* by Bernard Marshall, Appleton; *The Old Tobacco Shop: A True Account of What Befell a Little Boy in Search of Adventure* by William Bowen, Macmillan; *The Golden Fleece and the Heroes Who Lived before Achilles* by Padriac Colum, Macmillan; *Windy Hill* by Cornelia Meigs, Macmillan

1923 **Title:** *The Voyages of Doctor Dolittle*
Author: Hugh Lofting
Publisher: Frederick A. Stokes

1924 **Title:** *The Dark Frigate*
Author: Chares Hawes
Publisher: Atlantic Monthly Press

1925 **Title:** *Tales from Silver Lands*
Author: Charles Finger
Publisher: Doubleday, Page

Honor Books: *Nicholas: A Manhattan Christmas Story* by Anne Carroll Moore, G. P. Putnam's Sons; *Dream Coach* by Anne Parrish, Macmillan

1926 Title: *Shen of the Sea*
Author: Arthur Bowie Chrisman
Publisher: E. P. Dutton

Honor Book: *Voyagers* by Padraic Colum, Macmillan

1927 Title: *Smoky, the Cowhorse*
Author: Will James
Publisher: Charles Scribner's Sons

1928 Title: *Gayneck, the Story of a Pigeon*
Author: Dhan Gopal Mukerji
Publisher: E. P. Dutton

Honor Books: *The Wonder Smith and His Son: A Tale from the Golden Childhood of the World* by Ella Young, Longmans, Green; *Downright Dencey* by Caroline Snedeker, Doubleday

1929 Title: *The Trumpeter of Krakow*
Author: Eric P. Kelly
Publisher: Macmillan

Honor Books: *Pigtail of Ah Lee Ben Loo* by John Bennett, Longmans, Green; *Millions of Cats* by Wanda Gag, Coward-McCann; *The Boy Who Was* by Grace Hallock, E. P. Dutton; *Clearing Weather* by Cornelia Meigs, Little, Brown; *Runaway Papoose* by Grace Moon, Doubleday, Doran; *Tod of the Fens* by Elinor Whitney, Macmillan

1930 Title: *Hitty, Her First Hundred Years*
Author: Rachel Field
Publisher: Macmillan

Honor Books: *Daughter of the Seine: The Life of Madame Roland* by Jeanette Eaton, Harper and Brothers; *Pran of Albania* by Elizabeth Miller, Doubleday, Doran; *Jumping-Off Place* by Marian Hurd McNeely, Longmans, Green; *Tangle-Coated Horse and Other Tales: Episodes from the Fionn Saga* by Ella Young, Longmans, Green; *Vaino: A Boy of New England* by Julia Davis Adams, E. P. Dutton; *Little Blacknose* by Hildegarde Swift, Harcourt

1931 Title: *The Cat Who Went to Heaven*
Author: Elizabeth Coatsworth
Publisher: Macmillan

Honor Books: *Floating Island* by Anne Parrish, Harper and Brothers; *The Dark Star of Itza: The Story of a Pagan Princess* by Alida Malkus, Harcourt; *Queer Person* by Ralph Hubbard, Doubleday, Doran; *Mountains Are Free* by Julia Davis Adams, E. P. Dutton; *Spice and the Devil's Cave* by Agnes Hewes, Alfred A. Knopf; *Meggy Macintosh* by Elizabeth Janet Gray, Doubleday, Doran; *Garram the Hunter: The Boy of the Hill Tribes* by Herbert Best, Doubleday, Doran; *Ood-Le-Uk the Wanderer* by Alice Lide and Margaret Johansen, Little, Brown

1932 Title: *Waterless Mountain*
Author: Laura Adams Armer
Publisher: Longmans, Green

Honor Books: *The Fairy Circus* by Dorothy P. Lathrop, Macmillan; *Calico Bush* by Rachel Field, Macmillan; *Boy of the South Seas* by Eunice Tietjens, Coward-McCann; *Out of the Flame* by Eloise Lownsbery, Longmans, Green; *Jane's Island* by Marjorie Allee, Houghton Mifflin; *Truce of the Wolf and Other Tales of Old Italy* by Mary Gould Davis, Harcourt, Brace

1933 Title: *Young Fu of the Upper Yangtze*
Author: Elizabeth Foreman Lewis
Publisher: John C. Winston

Honor Books: *Swift Rivers* by Cornelia Meigs, Little, Brown; *The Railroad to Freedom: A Story of the Civil War* by Hildegarde Swift, Harcourt Brace; *Children of the Soil: A Story of Scandinavia* by Nora Burglon, Doubleday, Doran

1934 Title: *Invincible Louisa: The Story of the Author of Little Women*
Author: Cornelia Meigs
Publisher: Little, Brown

Honor Books: *The Forgotten Daughter* by Caroline Snedeker, Doubleday, Doran; *Swords of Steel* by Elsie Singmaster, Houghton Mifflin; *ABC Bunny* by Wanda Gag, Coward-McCann; *Winged Girl of Knossos* by Erik Berry, Appleton-Century; *New Land* by Sarah Schmidt, R. M. McBride; *Big Tree of Bunlahy: Stories of My Own Countryside* by Padraic Colum, Macmillan; *Glory of the Seas* by Agnes Hewes, Alfred A. Knopf; *Apprentice of Florence* by Ann Kyle, Houghton Mifflin

1935 Title: *Dobry*
Author: Monica Shannon
Publisher: Viking

Honor Books: *Pageant of Chinese History* by Elizabeth Seeger, Longmans, Green; *Davy Crockett* by Constance Rourke, Harcourt Brace; *Day on Skates: The Story of a Dutch Picnic* by Hilda Van Stockum, Harper

1936 Title: *Caddie Woodlawn*
Author: Carol Ryrie Brink
Publisher: Macmillan

Honor Books: *Honk, the Moose* by Phil Stong, Dodd, Mead; *The Good Master* by Kate Seredy, Viking; *Young Walter Scott* by Elizabeth Janet Gray, Viking; *All Sail Set: A Romance of the Flying Cloud* by Armstrong Sperry, John C. Winston

1937 Title: *Roller Skates*
Author: Ruth Sawyer
Publisher: Viking

Honor Books: *Phoebe Fairchild: Her Book* by Lois Lenski, Frederick A. Stokes; *Whistler's Van* by Idwal Jones, Viking; *Golden Basket* by Ludwig Bemelmans, Viking; *Winterbound* by Margery Bianco, Viking; *Audubon* by Constance Rourke, Harcourt, Brace; *The Codfish Musket* by Agnes Hewes, Doubleday, Doran

1938 Title: *The White Stag*
Author: Kate Seredy
Publisher: Viking

Honor Books: *Pecos Bill* by James Cloyd Bowman, Little, Brown; *Bright Island* by Mabel Robinson, Random House; *On the Banks of Plum Creek* by Laura Ingalls Wilder, Harper and Brothers

1939 Title: *Thimble Summer*
Author: Elizabeth Enright
Publisher: Rinehart

Honor Books: *Nino* by Valenti Angelo, Viking; *Mr. Popper's Penguins* by Richard and Florence Atwater, Little, Brown; *"Hello the Boat!"* by Phyllis Crawford, Henry Holt; *Leader by Destiny: George Washington, Man and Patriot* by Jeanette Eaton, Harcourt Brace; *Penn* by Elizabeth Janet Gray, Viking

1940 Title: *Daniel Boone*
Author: James Daugherty
Publisher: Viking

Honor Books: *The Singing Tree* by Kate Seredy, Viking; *Runner of the Mountain Tops: The Life of Louis Agassiz* by Mabel Robinson, Random House; *By the Shores of Silver Lake* by Laura Ingalls Wilder, Harper and Brothers; *Boy with a Pack* by Stephen W. Meader, Harcourt, Brace

1941 Title: *Call It Courage*
Author: Armstrong Sperry
Publisher: Macmillan

Honor Books: *Blue Willow* by Doris Gates, Viking; *Young Mac of Fort Vancouver* by Mary Jane Carr, Thomas Y. Crowell; *The Long Winter* by Laura Ingalls Wilder, Harper and Brothers; *Nansen* by Anna Gertrude Hall, Viking

1942 Title: *The Matchlock Gun*
Author: Walter D. Edmonds
Publisher: Dodd, Mead

Honor Books: *Little Town on the Prairie* by Laura Ingalls Wilder, Harper and Brothers; *George Washington's World* by Genevieve Foster, Charles Scribner's Sons; *Indian Captive: The Story of Mary Jemison* by Lois Lenski, Frederick A. Stokes; *Down Ryton Water* by Eva Roe Gaggin, Viking

1943 Title: *Adam of the Road*
Author: Elizabeth Janet Gray
Publisher: Viking

Honor Books: *The Middle Moffat* by Eleanor Estes, Harcourt, Brace; *Have You Seen Tom Thumb?* by Mabel Leigh Hunt, Frederick A. Stokes

1944 Title: *Johnny Tremain*
Author: Esther Forbes
Publisher: Houghton Mifflin

Honor Books: *The Happy Golden Years* by Laura Ingalls Wilder, Harper and Brothers; *Fog Magic* by Julia Sauer, Viking; *Rufus M.* by Eleanor Estes, Harcourt, Brace; *Mountain Born* by Elizabeth Yates, Coward-McCann

1945 Title: *Rabbit Hill*
Author: Robert Lawson
Publisher: Viking

Honor Books: *The Hundred Dresses* by Eleanor Estes, Harcourt, Brace; *The Silver Pencil* by Alice Dalgliesh, Charles Scribner's Sons; *Abraham Lincoln's World* by Genevieve Foster, Charles Scribner's Sons; *Lone Journey: The Life of Roger Williams* by Jeanette Eaton, Harcourt, Brace

1946 Title: *Strawberry Girl*
Author: Lois Lenski
Publisher: J. B. Lippincott

Honor Books: *Justin Morgan Had a Horse* by Marguerite Henry, Wilcox & Follett; *The Moved-Outers* by Florence Crannell Means, Houghton Mifflin; *Bhimsa, the Dancing Bear* by Christine Weston, Charles Scribner's Sons; *New Found World* by Katherine Shippen, Viking

1947 Title: *Miss Hickory*
Author: Carolyn Sherwin Bailey
Publisher: Viking

Honor Books: *Wonderful Year* by Nancy Barnes, J. Messner; *Big Tree* by Mary and Conrad Buff, Viking; *The Heavenly Tenants* by William Maxwell, Harper and Brothers; *The Avion My Uncle Flew* by Cyrus Fisher, Appleton-Century; *The Hidden Treasure of Glaston* by Eleanore Jewett, Viking

1948 Title: *The Twenty-One Balloons*
Author: William Pene du Bois
Publisher: Viking

Honor Books: *Pancakes-Paris* by Claire Huchet Bishop, Viking; *Le Lun, Lad of Courage* by Carolyn Treffinger, Abingdon-Cokesbury; *The Quaint and Curious Quest of Johnny Longfoot* by Catherine Besterman, Bobbs Merrill; *The Cow-tail Switch, and Other West African Stories* by Harold Courlander, Henry Holt; *Misty of Chincoteague* by Marguerite Henry, Rand McNally

1949 Title: *King of the Wind*
Author: Marguerite Henry
Publisher: Rand McNally

Honor Books: *Seabird* by Holling C. Holling, Houghton Mifflin; *Daughter of the Mountains* by Louis Rankin, Viking; *My Father's Dragon* by Ruth S. Gannett, Random House; *Story of the Negro* by Arna Bontemps, Alfred A. Knopf

1950 Title: *The Door in the Wall*
Author: Marguerite de Angeli
Publisher: Doubleday

Honor Books: *Tree of Freedom* by Rebecca Caudill, Viking; *The Blue Cat of Castle Town* by Catherine Coblentz, Longmans, Green; *Kildee House* by Rutherford Montgomery, Doubleday; *George Washington* by Genevieve Foster, Charles Scribner's Sons; *Song of the Pines: A Story of Norwegian Lumbering in Wisconsin* by Walter and Marion Havighurst, John C. Winston

1951 Title: *Amos Fortune, Free Man*
Author: Elizabeth Yates
Publisher: E. P. Dutton

Honor Books: *Better Known as Johnny Appleseed* by Mabel Leigh Hunt, J. B. Lippincott; *Gandhi, Fighter without a Sword* by Jeanette Eaton, Morrow; *Abraham Lincoln, Friend of the People* by Clara Ingram Judson, Wilcox & Follett; *The Story of Appleby Capple* by Anne Parrish, Harper

1952 Title: *Ginger Pye*
Author: Eleanor Estes
Publisher: Harcourt, Brace

Honor Books: *Americans before Columbus* by Elizabeth Baity, Viking; *Minn of the Mississippi* by Holling C. Holling, Houghton Mifflin; *The Defender* by Nicholas Kalashnikoff, Charles Scribner's Sons; *The Light at Tern Rock* by Julia Sauer, Viking; *The Apple and the Arrow* by Mary and Conrad Buff, Houghton Mifflin

1953 Title: *Secret of the Andes*
Author: Ann Nolan Clark
Publisher: Viking

Honor Books: *Charlotte's Web* by E. B. White, Harper; *Moccasin Trail* by Eloise McGraw, Coward-McCann; *Red Sails to Capri* by Ann Weil, Viking; *The Bears on Hemlock*

Mountain by Alice Dalgliesh, Charles Scribner's Sons; *Birthdays of Freedom*, Vol. 1, by Genevieve Foster, Charles Scribner's Sons

1954 Title: *. . . and now Miguel*
Author: Joseph Krumgold
Publisher: Thomas Y. Crowell

Honor Books: *All Alone* by Claire Huchet Bishop, Viking; *Shadrach* by Meindert DeJong, Harper; *Hurry Home, Candy* by Meindert DeJong, Harper; *Theodore Roosevelt, Fighting Patriot* by Clara Ingram Judson, Follett; *Magic Maize* by Mary and Conrad Buff, Houghton Mifflin

1955 Title: *The Wheel on the School*
Author: Meindert DeJong
Publisher: Harper

Honor Books: *The Courage of Sarah Noble* by Alice Dalgliesh, Charles Scribner's Sons; *Banner in the Sky* by James Ullman, J. B. Lippincott

1956 Title: *Carry on, Mr. Bowditch*
Author: Jean Lee Latham
Publisher: Houghton Mifflin

Honor Books: *The Secret River* by Marjorie Kinnan Rawlings, Charles Scribner's Sons; *The Golden Name Day* by Jennie Lindquist, Harper; *Men, Microscopes, and Living Things* by Katherine Shippen, Viking

1957 Title: *Miracles on Maple Hill*
Author: Virginia Sorensen
Publisher: Harcourt Brace

Honor Books: *Old Yeller* by Fred Gipson, Harper; *The House of Sixty Fathers* by Meindert DeJong, Harper; *Mr. Justice Holmes* by Clara Ingram Judson, Follett; *The Corn Grows Ripe* by Dorothy Rhoads, Viking; *Black Fox of Lorne* by Marguerite de Angeli, Doubleday

1958 Title: *Rifles for Watie*
Author: Harold Keith
Publisher: Thomas Y. Crowell

Honor Books: *The Horsecatcher* by Mari Sandoz, Westminister; *Gone-Away Lake* by Elizabeth Enright, Harcourt,

Brace; *The Great Wheel* by Robert Lawson, Viking; *Tom Paine, Freedom's Apostle* by Leo Gurko, Thomas Y. Crowell

1959 Title: *The Witch of Blackbird Pond*
Author: Elizabeth George Speare
Publisher: Houghton Mifflin

Honor Books: *The Family Under the Bridge* by Natalie Savage Carlson, Harper; *Along Came a Dog* by Meindert De-Jong, Harper; *Chucaro: Wild Pony of the Pampa* by Francis Kalnay, Harcourt, Brace; *The Perilous Road* by William O. Steele, Harcourt, Brace

1960 Title: *Onion John*
Author: Joseph Krumgold
Publisher: Thomas Y. Crowell

Honor Books: *My Side of the Mountain* by Jean George, E. P. Dutton; *America Is Born* by Gerald W. Johnson, Morrow; *The Gammage Cup* by Carol Kendall, Harcourt, Brace

1961 Title: *Island of the Blue Dolphins*
Author: Scott O'Dell
Publisher: Houghton Mifflin

Honor Books: *America Moves Forward* by Gerald W. Johnson, Morrow; *Old Ramon* by Jack Schaefer, Houghton Mifflin; *The Cricket in Times Square* by George Selden, Farrar, Straus

1962 Title: *The Bronze Bow*
Author: Elizabeth George Speare
Publisher: Houghton Mifflin

Honor Books: *Frontier Living* by Edwin Tunis, World; *The Golden Goblet* by Eloise McCraw, Coward-McCann; *Belling the Tiger* by Mary Stolz, Harper

1963 Title: *A Wrinkle in Time*
Author: Madeleine L'Engle
Publisher: Farrar, Straus

Honor Books: *Thistle and Thyme: Tales and Legends from Scotland* by Sorche Nic Leodhas, Holt, Rinehart, & Winston; *Men of Athens* by Olivia Coolidge, Houghton Mifflin

1964 Title: *It's Like This, Cat*
Author: Emily Cheney Neville
Publisher: Harper & Row

Honor Books: *Rascal* by Sterling North, E. P. Dutton; *The Loner* by Ester Wier, D. McKay

1965 Title: *Shadow of a Bull*
Author: Maia Wojciechowska
Publisher: Atheneum

Honor Book: *Across Five Aprils* by Irene Hunt, Follett

1966 Title: *I, Juan de Pareja*
Author: Elizabeth Borten de Trevino
Publisher: Farrar, Straus & Giroux

Honor Books: *The Black Cauldron* by Lloyd Alexander, Holt, Rinehart, & Winston; *The Animal Family* by Randall Jarrell, Pantheon; *The Noonday Friends* by Mary Stolz, Harper & Row

1967 Title: *Up a Road Slowly*
Author: Irene Hunt
Publisher: Follett

Honor Books: *The King's Fifth* by Scott O'Dell, Houghton Mifflin; *Zlateh the Goat and Other Stories* by Isaac Bashevis Singer, Harper & Row; *The Jazz Man* by Mary H. Weik, Atheneum

1968 Title: *From the Mixed-Up Files of Mrs. Basil E. Frankweiler*
Author: E. L. Konigsburg
Publisher: Atheneum

Honor Books: *Jennifer, Hecate, Macbeth, William McKinley, and Me, Elizabeth* by E. L. Konigsburg, Atheneum; *The Black Pearl* by Scott O'Dell, Houghton Mifflin; *The Fearsome Inn* by Isaac Bashevis Singer, Charles Scribner's Sons; *The Egypt Game* by Zilpha Keatley Synder, Atheneum

1969 Title: *The High King*
Author: Lloyd Alexander
Publisher: Holt, Rinehart, & Winston

Honor Books: *To Be a Slave* by Julius Lester, Dial; *When Shlemiel Went to Warsaw and Other Stories* by Isaac Bashevis Singer, Farrar, Straus & Giroux

1970 Title: *Sounder*
Author: William H. Armstrong
Publisher: Harper & Row

Honor Books: *Our Eddie* by Sulamith Ish-Kishor, Pantheon; *The Many Ways of Seeing: An Introduction to the Pleasures of Art* by Janet Gaylord Moore, World; *Journey Outside* by Mary Q. Steele, Viking

1971 Title: *Summer of the Swans*
Author: Betsy Byars
Publisher: Viking

Honor Books: *Kneeknock Rise* by Natalie Babbitt, Farrar, Straus & Giroux; *Enchantress from the Stars* by Sylvia Louise Engdahl, Atheneum; *Sing Down the Moon* by Scott O'Dell, Houghton Mifflin

1972 Title: *Mrs. Frisby and the Rats of NIMH*
Author: Robert C. O'Brien
Publisher: Atheneum

Honor Books: *Incident at Hawk's Hill* by Allan W. Eckert, Little, Brown; *The Planet of Junior Brown* by Virginia Hamilton, Macmillan; *The Tombs of Atuan* by Ursula K. Le Guin, Atheneum; *Annie and the Old One* by Miska Miles, Little, Brown; *The Headless Cupid* by Zilpha Keatley Snyder, Atheneum

1973 Title: *Julie of the Wolves*
Author: Jean Craighead George
Publisher: Harper & Row

Honor Books: *Frog and Toad Together* by Arnold Lobel, Harper & Row; *The Upstairs Room* by Johanna Reiss, Thomas Y. Crowell; *The Witches of Worm* by Zilpha Keatley Snyder, Atheneum

1974 Title: *The Slave Dancer*
Author: Paula Fox
Publisher: Bradbury

Honor Book: *The Dark is Rising* by Susan Cooper, Atheneum

1975 Title: *M. C. Higgins, the Great*
Author: Virginia Hamilton
Publisher: Macmillan

Honor Books: *Figgs & Phantoms* by Ellen Raskin, E. P. Dutton; *My Brother Sam is Dead* by James Lincoln Collier and Christopher Collier, Four Winds; *The Perilous Gard* by Elizabeth Marie Pope, Houghton Mifflin; *Philip Hall Likes Me, I Reckon Maybe* by Bette Greene, Dial

1976 Title: *The Grey King*
Author: Susan Cooper
Publisher: Atheneum

Honor Books: *The Hundred Penny Box* by Sharon Bell Mathis, Viking; *Dragonwings* by Laurence Yep, Harper & Row

1977 Title: *Roll of Thunder, Hear My Cry*
Author: Mildred D. Taylor
Publisher: Dial

Honor Books: *Abel's Island* by William Steig, Farrar, Straus & Giroux; *A String in the Harp* by Nancy Bond, Atheneum

1978 Title: *Bridge to Terabithia*
Author: Katherine Paterson
Publisher: Thomas Y. Crowell

Honor Books: *Ramona and Her Father* by Beverly Cleary, Morrow; *Anpao: An American Indian Odyssey* by Jamake Highwater, J. B. Lippincott

1979 Title: *The Westing Game*
Author: Ellen Raskin
Publisher: E. P. Dutton

Honor Book: *The Great Gilly Hopkins* by Katherine Paterson, Thomas Y. Crowell

1980 Title: *A Gathering of Days: A New England Girl's Journal 1830–32*
Author: Joan Blos

Publisher: Charles Scribner's Sons

Honor Book: *The Road from Home: The Story of an Armenian Girl* by David Kherdian, Morrow

1981 Title: *Jacob Have I Loved*
Author: Katherine Paterson
Publisher: Thomas Y. Crowell

Honor Books: *The Fledgling* by Jane Langton, Harper & Row; *A Ring of Endless Light* by Madeleine L'Engle, Farrar, Straus & Giroux

1982 Title: *A Visit to William Blake's Inn: Poems for Innocent and Experienced Travelers*
Author: Nancy Willard
Publisher: Harcourt Brace Jovanovich

Honor Books: *Ramona Quimby, Age 8* by Beverly Cleary, Morrow; *Upon the Head of the Goat: A Childhood in Hungary, 1939–1944* by Aranka Siegal, Farrar, Straus & Giroux

1983 Title: *Dicey's Song*
Author: Cynthia Voigt
Publisher: Atheneum

Honor Books: *Blue Sword* by Robin McKinley, Greenwillow; *Doctor DeSoto* by William Steig, Farrar, Straus & Giroux; *Graven Images* by Paul Fleischman, Harper & Row; *Homesick: My Own Story* by Jean Fritz, Putnam; *Sweet Whisper, Brother Rush* by Virginia Hamilton, Philomel

1984 Title: *Dear Mr. Henshaw*
Author: Beverly Cleary
Publisher: Morrow

Honor Books: *The Sign of the Beaver* by Elizabeth George Speare, Houghton Mifflin; *A Solitary Blue* by Cynthia Voigt, Atheneum; *The Wish Giver* by Bill Brittain, Harper & Row; *Sugaring Time* by Kathryn Lasky, Macmillan

1985 Title: *The Hero and the Crown*
Author: Robin McKinley
Publisher: Greenwillow

Honor Books: *Like Jake and Me* by Mavis Jukes, Alfred A.

Knopf; *The Moves Make the Man* by Bruce Brooks, Harper & Row; *One-Eyed Cat* by Paula Fox, Bradbury

1986 Title: *Sarah, Plain and Tall*
Author: Patricia MacLachlan
Publisher: Harper & Row

Honor Books: *Commodore Perry in the Land of the Shogun* by Rhoda Blumberg, Lothrop, Lee & Shepard; *Dogsong* by Gary Paulsen, Bradbury

1987 Title: *The Whipping Boy*
Author: Sid Fleischman
Publisher: Greenwillow

Honor Books: *A Fine White Dust* by Cynthia Rylant, Bradbury; *On My Honor* by Marion Dane Bauer, Clarion; *Volcano: The Eruption and Healing of Mount St. Helens* by Patricia Lauber, Bradbury

1988 Title: *Lincoln: A Photobiography*
Author: Russell Freedman
Publisher: Clarion

Honor Books: *After the Rain* by Norma Fox Mazer, Morrow; *Hatchet* by Gary Paulsen, Bradbury

1989 Title: *Joyful Noise: Poems for Two Voices*
Author: Paul Fleischman
Publisher: Harper & Row

Honor Books: *In the Beginning: Creation Stories from Around the World* by Virginia Hamilton, Harcourt Brace Jovanovich; *Scorpions* by Walter Dean Myers, Harper & Row

1990 Title: *Number the Stars*
Author: Lois Lowry
Publisher: Houghton Mifflin

Honor Books: *Afternoon of the Elves* by Janet Taylor Lisle, Orchard; *Shabanu, Daughter of the Wind* by Susan Fisher Staples, Alfred A. Knopf; *The Winter Room* by Gary Paulsen, Orchard

1991 Title: *Maniac Magee*
Author: Jerry Spinelli

Publisher: Little, Brown

Honor Book: *The True Confessions of Charlotte Doyle* by Avi, Orchard

1992 **Title:**   *Shiloh*
Author: Phyllis Reynolds Naylor
Publisher: Atheneum

Honor Books: *Nothing but the Truth* by Avi, Orchard; *Wright Brothers* by Russell Freedman, Holiday House

1993 **Title:**   *Missing May*
Author: Cynthia Rylant
Publisher: Orchard

Honor Books: *What Hearts* by Bruce Brooks, HarperCollins; *Dark Thirty: Southern Tales of the Supernatural* by Patricia C. McKissack, Alfred A. Knopf; *Somewhere in the Darkness* by Walter Dean Myers, Scholastic

1994 **Title:**   *The Giver*
Author: Lois Lowry
Publisher: Houghton Mifflin

Honor Books: *Crazy Lady!* by Jane Leslie Conly, Harper-Collins; *Dragon's Gate* by Laurence Yep, HarperCollins; *Eleanor Roosevelt: A Life of Discovery* by Russell Freedman, Clarion

1995 **Title:**   *Walk Two Moons*
Author: Sharon Creech
Publisher: HarperCollins

Honor Books: *Catherine, Called Birdy* by Karen Cushman, Clarion; *The Ear, the Eye, and the Arm* by Nancy Farmer, Orchard

1996 **Title:**   *The Midwife's Apprentice*
Author: Karen Cushman
Publisher: Clarion

Honor Books: *What Jamie Saw* by Carolyn Coman, Front Street; *The Watsons Go to Birmingham—1963* by Christopher Paul Curtis, Delacorte; *Yolanda's Genius* by Carol Fenner, Simon & Schuster; *The Great Fire* by Jim Murphy,

Scholastic

1997 Title: *The View from Saturday*
     Author: E. L. Konigsburg
     Publisher: Atheneum

Honor Books: *A Girl Named Disaster* by Nancy Farmer, Orchard; *Moorechild* by Eloise McGraw, Simon & Schuster; *The Thief* by Megal Whalen Turner, Greenwillow; *Belle Prater's Boy* by Ruth White, Farrar, Straus & Giroux

1998 Title: *Out of the Dust*
     Author: Karen Hesse
     Publisher: Scholastic

Honor Books: *Ella Enchanted* by Gail Carson Levine, HaperCollins; *Lily's Crossing* by Patricia Reilly Giff, Delacorte; *Wringer* by Jerry Spinelli, HarperCollins

1999 Title: *Holes*
     Author: Louis Sachar
     Publisher: Farrar, Straus & Giroux

Honor Book: *A Long Way from Chicago* by Richard Peck, Dial

ORBIS PICTUS AWARD AND HONOR BOOKS

The Orbis Pictus Award for Outstanding Nonfiction for Children, established by the National Council of Teachers or English in 1989, recognizes excellence in nonfiction writing for children. The name commemorates a 1657 publication *Orbis Pictus—The World in Pictures* by Johannes Amos Comenius, believed to be the first book actually planned for children.

1990 Title: *The Great Little Madison*
     Author: Jean Fritz
     Publisher: Putnam

Honor Books: *The Great American Gold Rush* by Rhoda Blumberg, Bradbury; *The News About Dinosaurs* by Patricia Lauber, Bradbury

1991 Title: *Franklin Delano Roosevelt*

Author: Russell Freedman
Publisher: Clarion

Honor Books: *Arctic Memories* by Normee Ekoomiak, Henry Holt; *Seeing Earth from Space* by Patricia Lauber, Orchard

1992 Title: *Flight: The Journey of Charles Lindbergh*
Authors: Robert Burleigh and Mike Wimmer
Publisher: Philomel

Honor Books: *Now Is Your Time! The African American Struggle for Freedom* by Walter Dean Myers, HarperCollins; *Prairie Vision: The Life and Times of Solomon Butcher* by Pam Conrad, HarperCollins

1993 Title: *Children of the Dust Bowl: The True Story of the School at Weedpatch Camp*
Author: Jerry Stanley
Publisher: Crown

Honor Books: *Talking with Artists* by Pat Cummings, Bradbury; *Come Back Salmon* by Molly Cone, Sierra Club

1994 Title: *Across America on an Emigrant Train*
Author: Jim Murphy
Publisher: Clarion

Honor Books: *To the Top of the World; Adventures with Arctic Wolves* by Jim Brandenburg, Walker & Company; *Making Sense: Animal Perception and Communication* by Bruce Brooks, Farrar, Straus & Giroux

1995 Title: *Safari beneath the Sea: The Wonder of the North Pacific Coast*
Author: Diane Swanson
Publisher: Sierra Club

Honor Books: *Wildlife Rescue: The Work of Dr. Kathleen Ramsay* by Jennifer Owings Dewey, Boyds Mill; *Kids at Work: Lewis Hine and the Crusade against Child Labor* by Russell Freedman, Clarion; *Christmas in the Big House, Christmas in the Quarters* by Patricia McKissack and Frederick McKissack, Scholastic

1996 Title: *The Great Fire*

Author: Jim Murphy
Publisher: Scholastic

Honor Books: *Dolphin Man: Exploring the World of Dolphins* by Laurence Pringle, photos by Randall S. Wells, Atheneum; *Rosie the Riveter: Women Working on the Home Front in World War II* by Penny Colman, Crown

1997 Title: *Leonardo da Vinci*
Author: Diane Stanley
Publisher: Morrow

Honor Books: *Full Steam Ahead: The Race to Build a Transcontinental Railroad* by Rhoda Blumberg, National Geographic Society; *The Life and Death of Crazy Horse* by Russell Freedman, Holiday House; *One World, Many Religions: The Way We Worship* by Mary Pope Osborne, Alfred A. Knopf

1998 Title: *An Extraordinary Life: The Story of a Monarch Butterfly*
Author: Laurence Pringle
Paintings: Bob Marstall
Publisher: Orchard

Honor Books: *A Drop of Water: A Book of Science and Wonder* by Walter Wick, Scholastic; *A Tree is Growing* by Arthur Dorros, illustrated by S. D. Schindler, Scholastic; *Charles A. Lindbergh: A Human Hero* by Jamees Cross Giblin, Clarion

1999 Title: *Shipwreck at the Bottom of the World: The Extraordinary True Story of Shackleton and the Endurance*
Author: Jennifer Armstrong
Publisher: Crown

Honor Books: *Black Whiteness: Admiral Byrd Alone in the Antarctic* by Robert Burleigh, illustrated by Walter Lyon Krudop, Atheneum, *Fossil Feud: The Rivalry of the First American Dinosaur Hunters* by Thom Holes, J. Messner; *Hottest, Coldest, Highest, Deepest* by Steve Jenkins, Houghton Mifflin; *No Pretty Pictures: A Child of War* by Anita Lobel, Greenwillow

Index

167